An Analysis of

William H. Whyte's

The Organization Man

Nikki Springer

Published by Macat International Ltd
24:13 Coda Centre, 189 Munster Road, London SW6 6AW.

Distributed exclusively by Routledge
2 Park Square, Milton Park, Abingdon, Oxon OX14 4RN
711 Third Avenue, New York, NY 10017, USA

Routledge is an imprint of the Taylor & Francis Group, an informa business

Copyright © 2018 by Macat International Ltd
Macat International has asserted its right under the Copyright, Designs and Patents Act
1988 to be identified as the copyright holder of this work.

www.macat.com
info@macat.com

Cataloguing in Publication Data
A catalogue record for this book is available from the British Library.
Library of Congress Cataloguing-in-Publication Data is available upon request.
Cover illustration: Angus Greig

ISBN 978-1-912453-47-4 (hardback)
ISBN 978-1-912453-02-3 (paperback)
ISBN 978-1-912453-17-7 (e-book)

Printed and bound by CPI Group (UK) Ltd, Croydon, CRO 4YY

Notice
The information in this book is designed to orientate readers of the work under analysis,
to elucidate and contextualise its key ideas and themes, and to aid in the development
of critical thinking skills. It is not meant to be used, nor should it be used, as a
substitute for original thinking or in place of original writing or research. References and
notes are provided for informational purposes and their presence does not constitute
endorsement of the information or opinions therein. This book is presented solely for
educational purposes. It is sold on the understanding that the publisher is not engaged
to provide any scholarly advice. The publisher has made every effort to ensure that
this book is accurate and up-to-date, but makes no warranties or representations with
regard to the completeness or reliability of the information it contains. The information
and the opinions provided herein are not guaranteed or warranted to produce particular
results and may not be suitable for students of every ability. The publisher shall not be
liable for any loss, damage or disruption arising from any errors or omissions, or from
the use of this book, including, but not limited to, special, incidental, consequential or
other damages caused, or alleged to have been caused, directly or indirectly, by the
information contained within.

CONTENTS

THE MACAT LIBRARY

The Macat Library is a series of unique academic explorations of seminal works in the humanities and social sciences – books and papers that have had a significant and widely recognised impact on their disciplines. It has been created to serve as much more than just a summary of what lies between the covers of a great book. It illuminates and explores the influences on, ideas of, and impact of that book. Our goal is to offer a learning resource that encourages critical thinking and fosters a better, deeper understanding of important ideas.

Each publication is divided into three Sections: Influences, Ideas, and Impact. Each Section has four Modules. These explore every important facet of the work, and the responses to it.

This Section-Module structure makes a Macat Library book easy to use, but it has another important feature. Because each Macat book is written to the same format, it is possible (and encouraged!) to cross-reference multiple Macat books along the same lines of inquiry or research. This allows the reader to open up interesting interdisciplinary pathways.

To further aid your reading, lists of glossary terms and people mentioned are included at the end of this book (these are indicated by an asterisk [*] throughout) – as well as a list of works cited.

Macat has worked with the University of Cambridge to identify the elements of critical thinking and understand the ways in which six different skills combine to enable effective thinking.
Three allow us to fully understand a problem; three more give us the tools to solve it. Together, these six skills make up the **PACIER** model of critical thinking. They are:

ANALYSIS – understanding how an argument is built
EVALUATION – exploring the strengths and weaknesses of an argument
INTERPRETATION – understanding issues of meaning

CREATIVE THINKING – coming up with new ideas and fresh connections
PROBLEM-SOLVING – producing strong solutions
REASONING – creating strong arguments

To find out more, visit **WWW.MACAT.COM.**

CRITICAL THINKING AND *THE ORGANIZATION MAN*

Primary critical thinking skill: CREATIVE THINKING
Secondary critical thinking skill: ANALYSIS

William Whyte's core idea in *The Organization Man* is that the Protestant Ethic that characterized financial and personal success in American history had been replaced in modern times by the Social Ethic. This stressed the group as the source of creativity and emphasized that the greatest need of the individual is to belong to a group. To investigate this idea, Whyte spent years interviewing the CEOs of Fortune 500 companies when he was an editor at *Fortune* magazine, one of the top business publications in the United States at the time. What he found was that the recruitment and training were much more focused on "cultural fit" than on technical skill or experience level.

As the ranks of new junior executives grew in post-World War II America, so did their impact on urban development and consumer spending. Droves of "package suburbs" sprang up in the fields surrounding major metropolitan areas, and a strong post-war economy coupled with funding from the GI Bill made new homes, cars, and household goods affordable for young families.

What makes *The Organization Man* so successful is Whyte's ability to capture so closely the essence, drivers, and larger impacts of the cultural shift he identified. Whyte did more than write a book. He coined a term and personified a generation of "Organization Men" who were not just middle-class businessmen, but emblematic of the golden age of capitalism and American history.

ABOUT THE AUTHOR OF THE ORIGINAL WORK

William Hollingsworth Whyte, Jr. (1917–1999) was an editor at
Fortune magazine, consultant to the New York City Planning
Commission, and later a Distinguished Professor at Hunter College in
New York City. He is the author of a number of notable publications on
urban planning topics, including *The Social Life of Small Urban Spaces*, *The
Last Landscape*, and *City: Rediscovering the Center*. The Project for Public
Spaces was founded in 1975 to advance the work and methods
developed by Whyte.

ABOUT THE AUTHOR OF THE ANALYSIS

Nikki Johnson Springer is currently a joint MBA and PhD Student at
Yale University. Her dissertation focuses on the development of
utility-scale solar energy on public lands in the American Southwest and
the competing needs of industry incentives, habitat conservation, and
federal regulation. Nikki is the former Garvan Chair & Visiting Professor
in Landscape Architecture at the University of Arkansas and has worked
in design and sustainability roles for Walmart and the Walt Disney
Company. She holds a Master of Landscape Architecture and Master of
Urban Planning from Harvard University and a Bachelor of Science in
Architecture from the Massachusetts Institute of Technology.

ABOUT MACAT

GREAT WORKS FOR CRITICAL THINKING

Macat is focused on making the ideas of the world's great thinkers
accessible and comprehensible to everybody, everywhere, in ways that
promote the development of enhanced critical thinking skills.

It works with leading academics from the world's top universities to
produce new analyses that focus on the ideas and the impact of the most
influential works ever written across a wide variety of academic disciplines.
Each of the works that sit at the heart of its growing library is an enduring
example of great thinking. But by setting them in context – and looking
at the influences that shaped their authors, as well as the responses they
provoked – Macat encourages readers to look at these classics and
game-changers with fresh eyes. Readers learn to think, engage and
challenge their ideas, rather than simply accepting them.

'Macat offers an amazing first-of-its-kind tool for interdisciplinary learning and research. Its focus on works that transformed their disciplines and its rigorous approach, drawing on the world's leading experts and educational institutions, opens up a world-class education to anyone.'

Andreas Schleicher
Director for Education and Skills, Organisation for Economic Co-operation and Development

'Macat is taking on some of the major challenges in university education … They have drawn together a strong team of active academics who are producing teaching materials that are novel in the breadth of their approach.'

Prof Lord Broers,
former Vice-Chancellor of the University of Cambridge

'The Macat vision is exceptionally exciting. It focuses upon new modes of learning which analyse and explain seminal texts which have profoundly influenced world thinking and so social and economic development. It promotes the kind of critical thinking which is essential for any society and economy. This is the learning of the future.'

Rt Hon Charles Clarke, former UK Secretary of State for Education

'The Macat analyses provide immediate access to the critical conversation surrounding the books that have shaped their respective discipline, which will make them an invaluable resource to all of those, students and teachers, working in the field.'

Professor William Tronzo, University of California at San Diego

WAYS IN TO THE TEXT

KEY POINTS

- Whyte was an American writer and urbanist* who made significant contributions to the literature of business and urban development.

- *The Organization Man* is the result of a series of interviews with corporate CEOs Whyte conducted while at *Fortune* magazine.

- The book makes the argument that post-World War II corporate culture was one of collectivism, in contrast to the individualism of historic America.

Who Was William H. Whyte?

William Hollingsworth Whyte was an American journalist and author. He was born on October 1, 1917 in West Chester, Pennsylvania and known to his friends and family as "Holly." Whyte attended high school at the St. Andrew's School in Middleton, Delaware before matriculating at Princeton University, and graduated in 1939. He joined the United States Marine Corps in 1941 and served at Guadalcanal (Solomon Islands) in World War II, advancing to the rank of Captain. Upon his return from service, he took a job with *Fortune* magazine.[1]

It was during his time at *Fortune* that Whyte began to explore the post–World War II corporate culture and the ways in which employees entered and advanced within an organization. This research, funded and supported by *Fortune*, directly contributed to his seminal work, *The Organization Man*. Toward the end of *The Organization Man*, Whyte began to explore the impacts of the new corporate culture on the families, homes, and communities of post-war executives. This inquiry was the bridge between his business research and his later work on urbanism and urban development. He left *Fortune* in 1958 and went on to make equally significant and compelling contributions to urban theory and the design of public spaces in America. Whyte died in New York City on January 12, 1999, at the age of 81.[2]

What Does *The Organization Man* Say?

The Organization Man describes and critiques the corporate culture of post-World War II America, its effects on the middle class, and the impact that culture had on the development of original and creative thought during the post-War period. Much of the material for the book came from primary sources, including more than 30 interviews with CEOs at *Fortune* 500 companies. Whyte's main conclusion was that a "Social Ethic" of conformity, cooperation, and stability had replaced the "Protestant Ethic" of those business tycoons such as railroad and banking executives who had dominated the Industrial Revolution* during the previous century. He introduced the concept of "Group Think" and the idea that, to succeed in their careers, employees had to subscribe to the predominant culture of the corporation at the cost of individualism, true excellence, and raw creativity. Whyte believed this shift to be a permanent one.

Whyte describes the Organization Man as having abandoned the Protestant Ethic of hard work, self-reliance, and thrift. He replaced it with a more modern Social Ethic, focused on fostering cooperation and a sense of belonging. He notes the changing focus of college graduates and corporate recruiting programs in response to this new Social Ethic. *The Organization Man* also provides an account of

Whyte's own experiences in the Vick Chemical Company and advises [then] current "organization men" on how to successfully navigate the complex and sometimes self-contradictory world of large, bureaucratic organizations. He warns, "Fight the organization. But not self-destructively."[3] Whyte recognizes that success within a company depends largely upon one's ability to fit within the existing culture.

In the second half of the book, Whyte explores how this dramatic shift in workplace culture also prompted significant changes in the personal lives of Organization Men and their families, finances, and home environment. He identifies dramatic shifts in the moral opinion of personal saving and spending, patterns in social groups and community involvement, trends in relocation and geographic demographics and the description of "package suburbs" where Organization Men and their families tended to live and socialize. *The Organization Man*, a study of "the ones of our middle class who have left home, spiritually as well as physically, to take the vows of organization life … who are the mind and soul of our great self-perpetuating institutions."[4]

Many identify *The Organization Man* as one of the first and most influential books in the field of business and management. However, it is also relevant beyond the business context, as a key piece of historical and cultural scholarship that serves as an ethnographic study of post-World War II America. Originally published in 1956, *The Organization Man* has sold more than two million copies.[5] Subsequent editions were published in 1972 and again most recently in 2002 with an updated introduction by Joseph Nocera,* who, like Whyte, was a former editor at *Fortune* Magazine.

Why Does *The Organization Man* Matter?

The Organization Man was one of the first critiques of the booming growth in large corporations in the post-World War II economy in the United States how that growth influenced family life, community development, and scientific discovery. Mark Carnes,* author of *The Columbia History of Post-World War II America* claims it to be "arguably the most popular sociological tract of the twentieth century."[6]

Whyte presents the culture of large corporations as directly in opposition to such core American ideals as independence, creative thought, and personal drive. In contrast, he describes "The Organization" as a place of compliance, complacency, and overwhelming bureaucracy. Perhaps even more concerning is that Whyte shows the spread of this trend to academic and scientific organizations such as universities and research laboratories. In places where innovation, intense creativity, and "thinking outside the box," matter the most, a business-oriented culture now has the power to rob the world of potential game-changing discoveries.

The Organization Man remains relevant to business and academic culture today. Whyte's identification of the "group think" mentality taking hold within America's foremost corporations is presented in stark contrast to the "rugged individualism" so ingrained in American history. He cautions readers to be aware of this change and to resist it, where appropriate, so as not to lose the importance of individualism in a burgeoning culture of conformity.

The entrepreneurial culture of tech start-ups often stands in stark contrast to the culture of the large, bureaucratic companies that Whyte describes. However, as these start-up companies begin to grow, they often start to move in the same direction, particularly when it comes to the need to balance creativity and innovation with the managerial, legal, financial and pragmatic requirements of running any large organization.

Whyte's work also showcases the idea that the workplace environment can and does have a huge impact on the personal lives of employees, their families, their finances, and where they live and socialize. This is true regardless of the cultural particulars of the companies and is one of the reasons that *The Organization Man* is relevant to more than one field of scholarship, further securing its importance for current and future generations.

NOTES

1 Michael Kaufman, "'Organization Man' Author and Urbanologist, Is Dead at 81." *The New York Times*, January 13, 1999, http://www.nytimes.com/1999/01/13/arts/william-h-whyte-organization-man-author-and-urbanologist-is-dead-at-81.html?pagewanted=all&src=pm. Claudia Levy, "William Whyte Dies." *The Washington Post*, January 14, 1999. https://www.washingtonpost.com/archive/local/1999/01/14/william-whyte-dies/60436392-1f58-4fa3-a61a-1a6277d626bf/?utm_term=.111ccfc66f23.

2 Kaufman, "Author and Urbanist."

3 William Whyte, *The Organization Man* (New York: Simon and Schuster, 1956), 12.

4 Jonathan Yardley, "William Whyte, Man Of The Mid-Century." *The Washington Post,* January 18, 1999. https://www.washingtonpost.com/archive/lifestyle/1999/01/18/william-whyte-man-of-the-mid-century/608a4308-4551-44b0-a17c-d0aa46f44792/?utm_term=.7c4a230619e8.

5 Kaufman, "Author and Urbanist."

6 Mark Carnes, *The Columbia History of Post-World War II America* (New York: Columbia University Press, 2012), 112.

SECTION 1
INFLUENCES

MODULE 1
THE AUTHOR AND THE HISTORICAL CONTEXT

KEY POINTS

* *The Organization Man* remains one of the leading critiques of corporate culture and the importance of the Social Ethic in business arena.

* Whyte's participation in the Vick School of Applied Merchandising gave him a personal insight into conformist corporate culture.

* Whyte's role at *Fortune* magazine put him in a unique position to observe and critique the inner world of large American corporations.

Why Read This Text?

Much of what the American middle class experiences at their place of employment was first identified and brought to light by Whyte in *The Organization Man*, and it remains relevant to this day. His book outlines the strategies for stable and sustainable employment in *Fortune* 500 corporations in post-World War II America and shows how these strategies carry over into personal finance and family life and even suburban and housing development.

The Organization Man is also a key piece of mid-twentieth century American history. The nation saw huge demographic and economic changes in the 1950s as soldiers returned home, married their long-distance sweethearts, mortgaged houses, started families, and joined the corporate workforce. "The America of the 1950s is so distant as to seem unrecognizable: its white-bread society and politics, its pre-computerized technology, its saccharine pre-rock-and-roll popular

> **❝ The book struck a chord in a nation that was undergoing deep changes, few of which it really understood, and it became a bestseller. ❞**
>
> Jonathan Yardley, "William Whyte, Man Of The Mid-Century" *Washington Post*

culture, its post–World War II cockiness and Cold War* vulnerability."[1]

While some claim *The Organization Man* is outdated, others see the culture of the workplace as cyclical and predict the return of Organization Men (and women)[2] as the United States reacts to the Great Recession,* an increased risk of nuclear war, an uncertain future for health care, and the rising costs of purchasing a home. At some point in the future, the pendulum of conformity and stability may well start to swing back toward the willing sacrifice of individual passion for stability and conformity.

Author's Life

William Hollingsworth "Holly" Whyte was born in 1917 in Pennsylvania, USA. After graduating from Princeton University, he joined the Vick Chemical Company and was a part of Vick's School of Applied Merchandising, a large corporate training program for incoming junior employees. Whyte's participation in this program introduced him to the ways in which large corporations train and assimilate new employees into the organization. This program would prove to be extremely influential in providing him with the initial idea, and perspective, for *The Organization Man*.[3]

Whyte stayed with Vick for two years before joining the US Marine Corps in 1941 to serve in World War II. On his return home in 1946, he joined *Fortune,* an American business magazine, notable for publishing a number of "long, thoughtful essays from contributors as diverse, and intellectual, as Daniel Bell, Galbraith and James Burnham."[4]

After publication of *The Organization Man*, Whyte shifted his focus to urban theory and design,* and later partnered with Jane Jacobs,* one of the most notable urban sociologists of the time and author of *The Death and Life of Great American Cities.*

Whyte married Jenny Bell Bechtel,* a fashion designer, in 1964. The couple had one daughter Alexandra Whyte. Jenny died of cancer in 2002 at age 75.[5]

Author's Background

Whyte came of age in the in the post-World War II era, a time commonly referred to as a "golden age" in American history. In the 1950s, Americans enjoyed a period of peace, prosperity, and progress. The economic markets were strong and the federal government poured resources into education and scientific research, fueling further growth in public corporations. Servicemen, returning home from the war, enrolled in college and bought houses in record numbers, both patterns supported by large government subsidy programs, such as the GI Bill* and the VA Loan Program.* As a result of these demographic and policy changes, large corporations, such as General Electric (GE), Radio Corporation of America (RCA), Ford, General Motors, Dow Chemical, and Vick Chemical, hired many young men into junior executive training programs.[6]

Whyte's work at *Fortune* magazine gave him a direct insight into the 1950s business culture. The magazine was described at the time as covering "business both in and of itself and as a part of the larger American culture."[7] Some have wrongly pegged Whyte as a social liberal working and writing in a conservative environment. In fact, Whyte himself was an Organization Man and had grown up in much the same type of environment he wrote about. Described as a "straight Establishment and a card-carrying, socially conservative member of the American gentleman class,"[8] Whyte was at home in the large corporations he profiled, and subject to much of the same training, testing, and scrutiny as were the other "Organization Men" he depicted.

In 1952, he published his first book, *Is Anybody Listening? How and why U.S. Business Fumbles When it Talks with Human Beings*, described in a *New York Times* book review as "an inquiry … into a massive failure of American business."[9] Whyte also published sections of what would later become *The Organization Man* as articles in *Fortune* in the early 1950s.

NOTES

1   Jonathan Yardley, "William Whyte, Man Of The Mid-Century," *The Washington Post*, January 18, 1999, https://www.washingtonpost.com/archive/lifestyle/1999/01/18/william-whyte-man-of-the-mid-century/608a4308-4551-44b0-a17c-d0aa46f44792/?utm_term=.7c4a230619e8.

2   Donna Randall, "Commitment and the Organization: The Organization Man Revisited," *Academy of Management Review*, 1987, Vol. 12, No. 3, 460-471.

3   Yardley, "Man of the Mid-Century."

4   Godfrey Hodgson, "Secret Life of US Corporations," *The Guardian*, January 15, 1999, https://www.theguardian.com/news/1999/jan/15/guardianobituaries1.

5   "Jenny Bechtel Whyte, Fashion Designer, 75," *The New York Times, September 4, 2002,* http://www.nytimes.com/2002/09/04/nyregion/jenny-bechtel-whyte-fashion-designer-75.html.

6   Gary Sernovitz, "What "The Organization Man" Can Tell Us About Inequality Today," *The New Yorker*, December 29, 2016, http://www.newyorker.com/business/currency/what-the-organization-man-can-tell-us-about-inequality-today.

7   Yardley, "Man of the Mid-Century."

8   Hodgson, "Secret Life."

9   David Cohn, "Ballyhoo And Faith; IS ANYBODY LISTENING? How and Why U. S. Business Fumbles When It Talks With Human Beings," *The New York Times*, April 6, 1952, http://www.nytimes.com/1952/04/06/archives/ballyhoo-and-faith-is-anybody-listening-how-and-why-u-s-business.html.

MODULE 2
ACADEMIC CONTEXT

KEY POINTS

- Business Management literature is concerned primarily with identifying ways that companies can be more productive and achieve their goals.

- Post-World War II corporations crafted a shift from "rugged and thrifty" individual employees to "well-rounded" team participants.

- As a former junior executive, Whyte was a member of the new "Organization Men" cohort, as well as a critic on the topic.

The Work in its Context

Post–World War II American culture and domestic life was one of conformity, peace, and prosperity under the leadership of Dwight D. Eisenhower,* a retired military hero who served as President of the United States of America between 1952–1960. A combination of economic incentives targeted at returning veterans helped this generation of ex-military men to attend college and purchase homes cheaply and en masse. Rising wages, a stable economy, and the baby boom* launched America into a strong middle-class family and consumer culture that persists today. The value of thrift had given way to a focus on consumption and the budding idea of "keeping up with the Joneses."[1]

Along with these prosperous times came a trend toward conformity, especially in the business world. Many GI's* graduating from college in the early 1950s were recruited into *Fortune* 500 corporations and understood the strict expectations of corporate culture. IBM is even

> **❝** Recognized as a benchmark, Whyte's book reveals the dilemmas at the heart of the group ethos that emerged in the corporate and social world of the postwar era. **❞**
>
> Nathan Glazer, *The Organization Man*

rumored to have required all men to wear white button-down shirts on a daily basis, though the company's webpage insists there was never a required "uniform."[2] Popular contemporary characterizations, as well as historical photographs of both government and corporate mid-century employees show employees–almost exclusively men at the time–dressed in a monotonous sea of grey and black suits.

The Organization Man was targeted primarily at the general public rather than academic audiences, though the book has come to be a core text in many history and business programs.[3] Although typically considered a business book, Whyte's work is as much an ethnographic study of a particular culture as it is an early entry into management literature. Whyte built on the work of German sociologist Max Weber* (1864–1920), who is most noted for his book *The Protestant Ethic and the Spirit of Capitalism*, published in 1905, which traced the link between the Protestant religion and capitalist ideas of secular work which fueled modern capitalism,* and ultimately, consumerism.*

Overview of the Field

Whyte had no formal background or academic training in anthropology, history, or even business or management scholarship, and nor was there a body of established intellectual thinkers or well-published authors on this subject at the time he was researching and writing. Whyte was, in many ways, a trailblazer both in the field of business management literature and in the growing number of authors commenting on the complacency and conformity of post-World War II American culture.

Whyte was, however, an experienced business writer at *Fortune* magazine, which at the time was one of the most prominent business publications in America. Whyte combined this background in business journalism with the growing number of critiques from sociology and history scholars and pop culture artists. "Whyte has fleshed out the well-known bones with up-to-the-minute detail."[4]

The Organization Man drew upon the cultural critiques that began in the 1940s and 1950s from such Frankfurt School* writers in Germany as Theodor Adorno,* Walter Benjamin,* Erich Fromm,* and Max Horkheimer.* They saw the negative aspects of capitalization and mass culture and sought to identify other aspects of social change. Their focus on the rising domination of large bureaucracies in capitalist societies and the loss of small-scale capitalism is a theme that is particularly relevant to *The Organization Man*. While the critiques of the Frankfurt School tended to be primarily pessimistic, Whyte's work on *The Organization Man* was considered to be as much a survival guide as it was a critique. He wanted his fellow Organization Men to thrive in their large bureaucracies by better understanding the curious new circumstances of their employment.

Academic Influences

The Organization Man was, and still is, considered a classic critique on the post-war American corporate culture and the rise of a conformist society. It was published along with a number of similar critiques and together they form a collective vision of the transformation of American society from one based on the self-reliant Protestant Ethic to a more socialistic collectivism.[5]

Of these contemporary works, the novel (and later film) *The Man in the Grey Flannel Suit* is one of the most popular, and lives long in cultural memory. *Chicago Tribune* newspaper columnist Bob Greene wrote that "the title became part of the American vernacular—the book was a ground-breaking fictional look at conformity in the executive suite, and it was a piece of writing that helped the nation's business community start to examine the effects of its perceived stodginess and sameness."[6] Whyte's publication of *The Organization Man* a year later provided a nonfiction confirmation of many of the concepts Wilson described in his novel. *The Man in the Grey Flannel Suit* "helped put a finger on what was bothering stressed white–collar professionals … that total submission of individualism to the aims of a large organization was not necessarily social progress."[7]

NOTES

1   James Patterson, *Grand Expectations: The United States, 1945-1974*, (New York: Oxford University Press, 1996), 312-317.

2   "The way we wore: A century of IBM attire," IBM Archives, Accessed October 2, 2017, https://www-03.ibm.com/ibm/history/exhibits/waywewore/waywewore_1.html.

3   Jonathan Yardley, "William Whyte, Man Of The Mid-Century." *The Washington Post,* January 18, 1999. https://www.washingtonpost.com/archive/lifestyle/1999/01/18/william-whyte-man-of-the-mid-century/608a4308-4551-44b0-a17c-d0aa46f44792/?utm_term=.7c4a230619e8.

4   C. Wright Mills, "Crawling to the Top," review of *The Organization Man by William H. Whyte, The New York Times, December 9, 1956.* http://www.nytimes.com/1956/12/09/archives/crawling-to-the-top-crawling-to-the-top.html.

5   Claudia Levy, "William Whyte Dies," *The Washington Post*, January 14, 1999, https://www.washingtonpost.com/archive/local/1999/01/14/william-whyte-dies/60436392-1f58-4fa3-a61a-1a6277d626bf/?utm_term=.111ccfc66f23.

6   Bob Greene, "A Lesson On What`s Inside The Suit," *The Chicago Tribune*, January 8, 1992, http://articles.chicagotribune.com/1992-01-08/features/9201020859_1_executive-suite-rich-magazine-story.

7   Levy, "William Whyte Dies."

MODULE 3
THE PROBLEM

KEY POINTS

- American and international scholars recognized a shift in society from one of individual determinism to one of rational conformism.

- Whyte defined the "Organization Man" by his willing loss of individualism for the stable but dull life of a corporate employee.

- Whyte provided a detailed portrait of the larger social theories gaining prominence in social and cultural critiques of the time.

Core Question

While there is some debate over Whyte's initial motivation in his research and publication of *The Organization Man*, he certainly made a major contribution to the social critiques of the Frankfurt School, the growing dominance of large corporations over business and everyday life, and the trend toward mass conformity in the 1950s. Whyte was himself an Organization Man and had a strong interest in understanding social behavior and the relationship between social structure and urban development.

The main and most controversial point of *The Organization Man* is that American companies, and America itself, were no longer being run by the "rugged individuals" so popular in the country's history, who rolled up their sleeves and relentlessly pursued hard work and innovation to be ultimately rewarded with wealth, prestige, and self-satisfaction. They had been replaced by the "Organization Men." In addition to the impacts on business and management of this change of

> ❝ This book is about the organization man. If the term is vague, it is because I can think of no other way to describe the people I am talking about. ❞
>
> William H. Whyte, *The Organization Man*

culture, Whyte explores its ripple effects on family dynamics, community stability, and suburban development.

To gather source information for his book, Whyte conducted numerous interviews with corporate CEOs and leaders of *Fortune* 500 companies. He discovered that one of their more alarming characteristics was that they identified themselves as part of their organization more than as individuals, and that this commitment to the organization was over and above, and sometimes at the expense of, their personal and family lives.

"Whyte thought that the old Protestant ethic—'that pursuit of individual salvation through hard work, thrift and competitive struggle'—was in a losing battle against the great organizations, or bureaucracies, that sheltered people who saw 'between themselves and organization … an ultimate harmony,' who subscribed to a 'social ethic' whose 'major propositions are three: a belief in the group as the source of creativity; a belief in belongingness as the ultimate need of the individual; and a belief in the application of science to achieve the belongingness'."[1]

The Participants

The main competing theory on workforce determination at the time was the Protestant Ethic and this stemmed largely from the work of German sociologist Max Weber. Whyte developed his contrasting 'Social Ethic' through one-on-one interviews that he drew together into generalized conclusions. This Social Ethic, he concluded, had supplanted the Protestant Ethic within the middle-class workforce.

However, says Venkatesh Rao, Whyte is not a serious academic: "Note though that it is not the careful opinions of these philosophers that Whyte thinks matters, but the crude and bastardized forms in which they diffused through the culture."[2]

Whyte's work drew on academic theorists, corporate executives, government officials, and mass media authors and appealed to both academic thinkers and the general public. The general consensus on the period Whyte explored was not one of competing theories, but one of multiple, nuanced, and similarly argued critiques of a general but unmistakable trend in business, society, and urban development.

Whyte's work, however, was unique it its approach and form. It was the catalyst for a number of subsequent critiques by scholars, literary and visual artists, and even musicians. In the following two decades, the public saw a surge of novels, movies, photographs, and even songs that all embraced the themes highlighted by Whyte. He offered the pubic, as well as scholars and academics, something new. "Regarded as one of the most important sociological and business commentaries of modern times, *The Organization Man* developed the first thorough description of the impact of mass organization on American society."[3]

The Contemporary Debate

Whyte did more than write an account of 1950's corporate America. He coined a term and a concept that remains a powerful, succinct characterization of a large portion of middle class America that is at once sought-after and disdained. *The Organization Man* is more than a book title; it is a way of life. There is still a large overlap between how we identify and where we seek employment and the type of work we do. Whyte characterized the Organization Man as someone who prides himself, and associates himself, more with the company he works for than his individual background, interests, or areas of expertise.

Whyte is typically grouped together with other scholars of the time and gives a personal and detailed account of the theoretical, academic, and fictionalized versions of the "social ethic" argument. However, it is unclear how much he directly engaged with them. Rather, he was observing the same trends at the same time. Whyte doesn't specifically mention the Frankfurt School scholars or other contemporary social theory authors and limits such direct references to urban planning scholars such as Phil Klutznick* of the Urban Investment and Development Company. This is perhaps indicative of the urban focus of his later work, as Whyte "went on to a distinguished second career as a scholar of the human habitat, specifically as a close observer of street life and urban space."[4]

NOTES

1   Jonathan Yardley, "William Whyte, Man Of The Mid-Century," *The Washington Post*, January 18, 1999, https://www.washingtonpost.com/archive/lifestyle/1999/01/18/william-whyte-man-of-the-mid-century/608a4308-4551-44b0-a17c-d0aa46f44792/?utm_term=.7c4a230619e8.

2   Venkatesh Rao, "The Ideology of the Organization Man," *Ribbonfarm*, November 23, 2008, https://www.ribbonfarm.com/2008/11/23/the-ideology-of-the-organization-man/.

3   Joseph Nocera, Forward to *The Organization Man* (Philadelphia, University of Pennsylvania Press, 2013).

4   Michael Kaufman, "'Organization Man' Author and Urbanologist, Is Dead at 81." *The New York Times*, January 13, 1999, http://www.nytimes.com/1999/01/13/arts/william-h-whyte-organization-man-author-and-urbanologist-is-dead-at-81.html?pagewanted=all&src=pm.

MODULE 4
THE AUTHOR'S CONTRIBUTION

KEY POINTS

* Whyte's central thesis is the replacement of the Protestant Ethic with the Social Ethic as the path to economic and professional success.

* Whyte's work crystalized the idea of the social ethic and brought it to the public.

* Whyte's detailed descriptions gave real-world examples to the abstract critiques of the Frankfurt School and other contemporary writers.

Author's Aims

Whyte combined the nuanced information gleaned from personal one-on-one interviews with prominent CEOs and detailed, mostly objective observations on corporate culture, hiring practices, geographic trends, and suburban design to create a generation-defining ethnographic study of 1950s middle-class American culture. His aims, however, have been largely misunderstood, as many consider his work to be a subjective "scathing critique" of post-war conformity rather than the objective ethnographic research it actually is.

As Whyte states himself later in his career, "Some years ago I wrote a book about the people who work for large organizations. I called them organization men. Some people got mad at me for this. They said I was calling them dirty conformists. But I wasn't. I was an organization man myself (Vicks, Fortune magazine, the Marine Corps), and I meant no slight. Quite the contrary. My point was that these were the people who were running the country, not the rugged

> **66** *The Organization Man* is one of the most influential books of the twentieth century. It established the categories Americans now use when thinking about the workplace, the suburbs, and their lives. **99**
>
> David Brooks, *The Organization Man* (Back Cover)

individualists of American folklore. And that they had better beware of the bureaucratic ethic."[1]

The execution of Whyte's intentions is clear and thorough. He provides intimate details of the everyday life and overall career trajectory of the Organization Men he profiles, in some cases down to the minutest detail.

Whyte's goal was not to call for a mass overthrow of the new status quo he was observing and profiling, but to educate current and future Organization Men about how to succeed through such observations as "be smart, but not too smart,"[2] and the appendix on "How to Cheat on Personality Tests." His aim was to help Organization Men, and the public more broadly, about the changes in society and to encourage a level of awareness and skepticism about them.

Approach

Whyte's interest in exploring the changing nature of business in post-war America was piqued by his knowledge of the 1949 class graduating from Princeton University and other top-tier peer universities. Whyte noted that he was "surprised to find the absence of any cynicism about big organization life."[3] Whyte was struck by this acceptance because his own experience as a graduate of the Princeton class of 1939 was starkly different, described as being "mostly fired into cold hostility." Ten years later, graduates "go into a nice pleasant corporation extension of the campus in which everyone gets along, the instruction is in how to become a committee bureaucrat, and the career goal is not achievement or work but the management of *other* people's work."

This observation is fundamental to Whyte's work, and is confirmed over and over again in his interviews with corporate CEOs and mid-level managers. Whyte conducts as much of a 360-degree ethnographic profile as possible, observing the Organization Men in their places of business, within their homes and families, during their commutes, and in social and commercial (shopping) interactions.

Whyte's writing influenced other scholars in forming their own opinions, largely negative, of the period and its social trends. His description of Park Forest, Illinois, for example, noted the many ways in which Organization Men and their families engaged with neighbors and formed tight-knit social groups. However, many subsequent writers used his descriptions as evidence of just the opposite and portrayed a faceless, monotonous, isolated suburbia.[4]

Contribution in Context

Whyte's *Organization Man* is undeniably important in providing the groundwork and knowledge base for a wide variety of critiques on business, society, family dynamics, and suburban and regional development in the second half of the twentieth century. He built on the theoretical foundation of the Frankfurt School scholars, and delivered these ideas of conformity, groupthink, and the social ethic to the masses. Described as "Perhaps the most important work of suburban criticism of the 1950s," by professor and author Becky Nicolaides, she notes "his work had tremendous influences on subsequent suburban critics, journalists, novelists, filmmakers, and urban scholars, who portrayed suburbia as a place defined, above all, by conformity."[5] C. Wright Mills, a peer sociologist noted in 1956: "Mr. Whyte's book challenged and refuted claims of entrepreneurial vigor and daring in business by describing an ongoing bureaucratization of white-collar environments—board rooms, offices, laboratories."

The success of *The Organization Man* came as a surprise. It had a small first printing because the publisher doubted it would catch on. In fact, it quickly became a bestseller and stayed one for seven months.[6] Not only was it popular in its own right, it was the first of a large and notable trend in cultural critiques of the time. In the years immediately following its publication, its message was reinforced with numerous other fiction and nonfiction works of similar nature.

NOTES

1   William Whyte, "Organization Man Revisited," *The New York Times*, December 7, 1986, http:/www.nytimes.com/1986/12/07/magazine/ organization-man-revisited-the-organization-man-a-rejoinder.html.

2   Joseph Nocera, Forward to *The Organization Man* (Philadelphia: University of Pennsylvania Press, 2013).

3   William Whyte. *Princeton Alumni Weekly*, Vol. 57 (1957), 45.

4   Becky Nicolaides and Andrew Wiese, *The Suburb Reader* (New York: Taylor & Francis, 2006)

5   Nicolaides, *The Suburb Reader*.

6   Claudia Levy, "William Whyte Dies," *The Washington Post*, January 14, 1999, https:/www.washingtonpost.com/archive/local/1999/01/14/ william-whyte-dies/60436392-1f58-4fa3-a61a-1a6277d626bf/?utm_ term=.111ccfc66f23.

SECTION 2
IDEAS

MODULE 5
MAIN IDEAS

KEY POINTS

- Whyte describes the replacement of "rugged individualism" in American society by corporate conformity.

- The "group-think" culture that emerged in the 1950s is in direct opposition to the Protestant Ethic.

- The "Social Ethic" identified by Whyte is the idea that a sense of belonging and togetherness in a consensus-driven organization are more important than individual creativity.

Key Themes

The Organization Man introduced the reader to the standards and drivers of corporate culture in the post–World War II economy in America. The book is both a history and a critique of the high numbers of white, middle and upper class young male employees entering the corporate workforce after graduating from college in the 1950s.

Large corporations dominated this economy, many of which are still household names. However, success at these corporations typically required employees to subscribe to the newly emerging culture of group dynamics and passively accept the company's behavioural standards. These junior executives were groomed to manage, rather than to generate new ideas or challenge the status quo.

As described by Whyte in the introduction: "This book is about the organization man. If the term is vague, it is because I can think of no other way to describe the people I am talking about. They are not the workers, nor are they the white-collar people in the usual, clerk sense of the word. These people only work for The Organization ... they are of the staff as much as the line, and most are destined to

> **❝** The Organization Man,' sounded an early warning about spreading conformity in postwar America. **❞**
> Claudia Levy, "William Whyte Dies."

live poised in a middle area that still awaits a satisfactory euphemism. But they are the dominant members of our society nonetheless … and it is their values which will set the American temper."[1]

Exploring the Ideas

The clear difference in the business world discovered by the graduates of 1939 and 1949 was due, in large part Whyte noted, to "a rapid shift in thinking over the past few years, from the old 'Protestant Ethic' — meaning the old ideals of self-reliance, individual independence, thrift, ambition, by which the nation reached its present stature; to the new 'Social Ethic'… that contemporary body of thought which makes morally legitimate the pressures of society against the individual."[2]

The 'Social Ethic' Whyte defines as the "contemporary body of thought which makes morally legitimate the pressures of society against the individual. Its major propositions are three: a belief in the group as the source of creativity; a belief in 'belongingness' as the ultimate need of the individual; and a belief in the application of science to achieve that belongingness."[3]

In addition to the Social Ethic, there are a number of other important themes in the book. First, this corporate culture of conformity was quickly becoming congruent with American middle class culture more generally, with its respect for authority and desire to blend in and humble one's distinctions and accomplishments. Whyte identified the "fight against genius." An Organization Man needed to be good and smart, but not too good or too smart, and keep the peace at work and at home.

A necessary component of this ethic is the idea of "groupthink," a term Whyte coined in *The Organization Man*. Groupthink is the belief that the ultimate source of creativity is the group and the desire to belong to that group is the individual's ultimate need.[4] "Whyte argued for individualism within organization life." But he still saw a rebalancing of American values chipping away at Americans' human potential—and their happiness. Whyte observed the rising popularity of training programs emphasizing more democratic values, like the one at General Electric, where a young man was taught, "To get ahead, he must co-operate with the others—but co-operate better than they do."[5]

Along with massive peer pressure at work and at home–and supported by the strong post-war economy–came the loss of the Protestant ideas of savings and thrift. These were replaced by the consumer and family finance culture of saving for specific items and the development of revolving credit through department stores and low interest mortgages for more affordable suburban homes. Here, Whyte relies on the observations of Ernest Dichter, a market researcher (a relatively new occupation at the time): "We are now confronted with the problem of permitting the average American to feel moral even when he…is spending, even when he is not saving, even when he is taking two vacations a year and buying a second or third car. One of the basic problems of this prosperity, then, is to give people the sanction and justification to enjoy it and to demonstrate that the hedonistic approach to his life is a moral, not an immoral one.[6]

Language and Expression

Although *The Organization Man* was Whyte's first book, he was not an inexperienced writer. As an editor at *Fortune* magazine, Whyte developed the ability to write for a wide range of readers: business executives, academic minds, and the general public. This was the audience for *The Organization Man* as well. Whyte approaches his topics with a clear, almost perfunctory language style, free of gratuitous adjectives and flowery descriptions, making the book readily accessible to almost anyone—and this further contributed to its popularity.

Whyte coined a number of terms in the book, the most important among them the title phrase "Organization Man" itself. This phrase now appears in several dictionaries, including the 2012 Collins English Dictionary as "noun 1. a person who subordinates his personal life to the demands of the organization he works for; 2. a person who specializes in or is good at organization," and the 2005 American Heritage New Dictionary of New Cultural Literacy as "Someone who represses individual desires and molds behavior to conform to the demands of the organization he or she works for."

Other coined terms include "Groupthink": "noun: The practice of thinking or making decisions as a group, resulting typically in unchallenged, poor-quality decision-making" (OED, 2017), and the Social Ethic, as described previously.

NOTES

1   William Whyte, *The Organization Man* (New York: Simon & Schuster, 1956).

2   William Whyte. *Princeton Alumni Weekly*, Vol. 57 (1957), 45.

3   Whyte, *The Organization Man*.

4   Donna Randall, "Commitment and the Organization: The Organization Man Revisited," *Academy of Management Review*, 1987, Vol. 12, No. 3, 460-471, http://www.jstor.org/stable/pdf/258513.pdf?refreqid=excelsior%3A0a9742fe94fd6bf26211c59cc6f15745.

5   Gary Sernovitz, "What "The Organization Man" Can Tell Us About Inequality Today," *The New Yorker* (December 29, 2016), http://www.newyorker.com/business/currency/what-the-organization-man-can-tell-us-about-inequality-today.

6   Venkatesh Rao, "The Ideology of the Organization Man," *Ribbonfarm*, November 23, 2008, https://www.ribbonfarm.com/2008/11/23/the-ideology-of-the-organization-man/.

MODULE 6
SECONDARY IDEAS

KEY POINTS

- The main secondary idea in *The Organization Man* is that changes in business environments impact suburban development.

- Whyte notes that the organizational changes he described have occurred in academic and scientific research environments as well.

- Whyte also writes on the impacts organizational changes have had on relationships, families, and leisure time.

Other Ideas

The main secondary idea in Whyte's text is that the Organization Man has become detached from his hometown and upbringing, and substituted his participation in a transitory community of other unattached Organization Men who belong to their respective companies. On this point, Whyte highlights the necessary mobility of the Organization Men to go wherever the Organization needs them, often at little notice. "The Organization Man, wrote Whyte, "must not only accept control, he must accept it as if he liked it ... He must smile when he is transferred to a place or a job that isn't the job or place he happens to want ... he must be less 'goal-centered,' more 'employee-centered.' It is not enough now that he work hard; he must be a damn good fellow to boot."[1] Whyte also discusses the changes to overall creativity, pursuit of individual activities, and individual self-determination that he observes in Organization Men. "With the rise of the postwar corporation, American individualism had disappeared from the mainstream of middle-class life."[2]

> **❝** The Organization Man" made the point that total submission of individualism to the aims of a large organization was not necessarily social progress. **❞**
> Claudia Levy, "William Whyte Dies."

Whyte notes in an earlier article, *The Transients*, published in *Fortune* in 1953: "To visitors from older communities, the sight of rank after rank of little boxes stretching off to infinity, one hardly distinguishable from the other, is weird... What he has seen is the dormitory of the next managerial class... it may be the new suburban communities that provide the sharpest picture of tomorrow's management. Not only are managerial transients concentrated here, they are concentrated almost totally free of the pressures of older traditions and older people that would affect them elsewhere."

Exploring the Ideas

Whyte devotes a large section of his book to the suburban lifestyle of an Organization Man. He describes the newly-built communities that house them and their families, and they ways in which their design further supports many of the central themes of the book. Whyte also described, and mapped, some of the patterns of social interaction in these communities and noted how they supported a stable, middle-class upbringing for children in good school districts and fostered a certain type of community engagement that focused primarily on church groups and civic service.[3]

As the Organization Man advanced within the company, in addition to increased financial compensation, he was also expected to alter his personal and family life to support this corporate advancement, often with relocation assignments. The wives of corporate Organization Men often had their own share of duties, such as hosting dinners with key executives, and thus maintaining a home that would be acceptable for this type of entertaining, or forming friendships with the wives of other fellow employees. As Whyte stated, the Organization Man "must not only accept control, he must accept it as if he liked it."

The life of the "Organization Wife" is a necessary component of the overall "Organization" lifestyle. Whyte explained: "As for the wives of Organization Men, most wives agreed with the corporation; they too felt that the good wife is the wife who adjusts graciously to the system, curbs open intellectualism or the desire to be alone."[4] The wife of a successful, and advancing, junior executive, must be pleasant in appearance and figure, properly dressed, and maintain a proper home, not too fancy but not too simple, appropriate for hosting business dinners and civic social gatherings.

Whyte makes small reference to the sources of this generation's affinity for corporate bureaucracy, noting that the desire for stable, if boring, employment was driven by the uncertainty of the Great Depression and the fears of global destruction during World War II. It is not surprising that after those decades of high stress and uncertainty, Americas would willingly accept a stable, dull, non-confrontational life. "Having fought a 'good war,' they were embraced by an adoring public upon their return. Having come of age during the Depression, they were eager for prosperity, security and stability ... Determined to survive in the workplace, they submerged personal ambition and individualism in favor of corporate conformity."[5]

Overlooked

While Whyte is primarily concerned with the lives of corporate executives, he notes that this change from the Protestant to the Social Ethic has also impacted the scientific and academic communities, and that this impact is perhaps far more dangerous to humankind than the sterilization of creativity and individuality within public corporations. Scientific discovery, Whyte notes, is largely dependent on individual exploration, and in particular, by individuals who are unafraid to pursue radical or unorthodox ideas and who are unhindered by criticism from others: the exact qualities that were out of fashion for Organization Men. The same is true for academic discourse; one must be able to argue and defend a thesis against competing ideas. In later critiques of Whyte's work, relatively little is mentioned on this topic.

Whyte also notes the importance of personality testing as part of corporate recruiting, and advises the would-be Organization Man with very specific instructions as to how to "cheat" on the tests by "give[ing] the most conventional, run-of-the-mill, pedestrian answer possible."[6] He also notes the overall trend of increasing numbers of college graduates abandoning liberal arts degrees in favor of degrees in engineering or business, and how this is related to trends in corporate recruiting practices.

NOTES

1   Virginia Postrel, "Dialogue: How Has 'The Organization Man' Aged?; Nostalgia's Illusions," *The New York Times*, January 17, 1999, http://www. nytimes.com/1999/01/17/opinion/dialogue-how-has-the-organization-man-aged-nostalgia-s-illusions.html.

2   Postrel, "Dialogue."

3   William Whyte, *The Organization Man* (New York: Simon & Schuster, 1956), 369-381.

4   Michael Kaufman, "'Organization Man' Author and Urbanologist, Is Dead at 81," *The New York Times*, January 13, 1999, http://www.nytimes. com/1999/01/13/arts/william-h-whyte-organization-man-author-and-urbanologist-is-dead-at-81.html?pagewanted=all&src=pm.

5   Martha Groves, "Lessons From 'The Organization Man' Still Have Some Relevance for Today," *LA Times*, January 24, 1999, http://articles.latimes. com/1999/jan/24/business/fi-1115

6   Whyte, *The Organization Man, 196.*

MODULE 7
ACHIEVEMENT

KEY POINTS

- *The Organization Man* was an immediate bestseller and remains a classic and seminal text on business and management.

- The most important factor in Whyte's success was his ability to codify the trends he was observing in a way the public could understand.

- Some critics later argued that Whyte did not anticipate the future changes to workforce dynamics, such as layoffs and globalization.

Assessing the Argument

The Organization Man achieved great success and popularity soon after publication. This popularity was reflected in the numerous books and movies on similar themes of mid-century culture that appeared in the decades after its publication. Although some claim Whyte was overly critical of Organization Men (like himself), his message was clear: society must be educated and aware of the sacrifices it makes in exchange for the security and belongingness of corporate loyalty.

Whyte's success was due to several factors. One, that he was able to capture the tone and temperament of mainstream society with impeccable accuracy and explore it in numerous, seemly disparate ways. "His belief in the value of the individual mind lends an edge to his work, and makes his description of the ethos of the technician in America today among the best available … His account of the organization … is first rate."[1]

> **❝** Regarded as one of the most important sociological and business commentaries of modern times, *The Organization Man* developed the first thorough description of the impact of mass organization on American society. **❞**
>
> Joseph Nocera, *The Organization Man*

Additionally, Whyte's fame was supported by the many other authors, writers, and artists all circling around the same ideas of conformity, peer pressure, and individuality. Whyte was considered a leader in a large, popular critique of society. "A native tradition of self-questioning was revived by writers rooted in a socialist or radical liberal tradition. Whyte found himself lumped with them."[2]

Achievement in Context

The Organization Man is important for several reasons. First, it was the first-of-its kind portrayal of middle management, an increasingly important subset of the population in post-World War II America, fueling subsequent studies on employee motivation, talent planning, and workforce and organization dynamics. Whyte's work on the urban and suburban theory aspects of *The Organization Man* were so hghly regarded that sections of his work are included in the "America on the Move" exhibit at the Smithsonian National Museum of American History, a leading museum institution in the United States. Jay W. Lorsch, a Professor of Human Relations at Harvard Business School, agrees that Whyte "certainly coined a word and captured something, a very apt description of where we were at a particular point in time. Maybe it didn't change anything, but it made a point."[3]

Second, it brought the ideas of the Frankfurt School to the masses, and encouraged them to question critically the consequences of the life choices they were making in pursuit of stability, conformity, and security. "When a young man says that to make a living these days you must do what somebody else wants you to do, he states it not only as a fact of life that must be accepted but as an inherently good proposition."[4] Whyte fluidly brought together ideas of Marxism,* Scientism,* Capitalism, urban theories, labor theories,* and the nascent field of management literature* to produce a popular bestseller and cultural icon. "In the thirty years following World War II, management has been the essential human activity within modern organizations … But beneath that ostensible nobility of purpose lay two facts that no one – except a few cranky intellectuals – wanted to confront. The first was that the organization of America was killing individualism, pluralism, and community. The second was that, in our society, power accrues to those who control the major organizations."[5]

Third, it codified and crystalized an important element of popular culture, bringing the idea of the Organization Man into everyday language and thought. "We still remember the book sixty years later because half of it considers cultural changes outside the corporation: in the physical design, sociology, and marital dynamics of the new suburbs, in the practice of science, even in the era's novels. Whyte, in successive sections, shows people inside and outside their jobs, in thought and action, being influenced by the same cultural trend toward the Social Ethic—or trying to resist it."[6]

Limitations

The Organization Man has made notable contributions to several fields of academic discourse and influenced numerous cultural references. Whyte's work contributed to scholarly work in history, sociology, organizational dynamics,* business management, and urban theory, as well as in popular culture including novels, films, art, and photography. References to Whyte's characterization of corporate conformity can be seen in contemporary references as diverse as Mac/Apple commercials, the Emmy-winning television drama *Mad Men*, and *Dilbert* comics.[7]

Whyte's most obvious limitation was that he assumed this state of willing conformity and the prevailing Social Ethic would be permanent. He failed to note the overarching trend that trust in organizations and government tends to be cyclical and he could not have predicted some of the signature events of the 1960s, such as the Watergate scandal* and the Vietnam War,* both of which severely impacted, and destroyed, much of the Baby Boom generation's trust in government, and by extension, their trust in authority more generally.

"The implicit premise of the book was that the change was permanent: that the Organization Man and all he represented would henceforth define the American character. That Whyte's conformist organization represented the mature form of capitalism was conventional wisdom until fairly recently. Technology and capital markets had made entrepreneurship, and unpredictable economic evolution, obsolete."[8] As the circumstances of history, society, and culture have changed, so has *The Organization Man's* place of prominence but, regardless of the changes, Whyte's characterization has secured a generation-defining place in culture and cultural memory.

NOTES

1   C. Wright Mills, "Crawling to the Top," review of The Organization Man by William H. Whyte, *The New York Times*, December 9, 1956., http://www.nytimes.com/1956/12/09/archives/crawling-to-the-top-crawling-to-the-top.html

2   Godfrey Hodgson,. "Secret Life of US Corporations," *The Guardian*, January 15, 1999, https://www.theguardian.com/news/1999/jan/15/guardianobituaries1.

3   Martha Groves, "Lessons From 'The Organization Man' Still Have Some Relevance for Today," *LA Times*, January 24, 1999, http://articles.latimes.com/1999/jan/24/business/fi-1115.

4   Richard Koch, "The Rise & Fall Of Organization Man," *Huffington Post*,
     March 14, 2017, https://www.huffingtonpost.com/entry/the-rise-fall-of-
     organization-man_us_58c7ded1e4b0d06aa6580497

5   William Scott and David Hart, *Organizational values in America* (Transaction
     Publishers, 1989), 4.

6   Gary Sernovitz, "What "The Organization Man" Can Tell Us About Inequality
     Today," *The New Yorker, December 29, 2016.*   http://www.newyorker.com/
     business/currency/what-the-organization-man-can-tell-us-about-inequality-
     today.

7   David Leonard, "William Whyte's The Organization Man," *Bloomberg*,
     December 4, 2014, https://www.bloomberg.com/news/articles/2014-12-04/
     the-organization-man-conformity-of-corporate-culture-revealed.

8   Virginia Postrel, "Dialogue: How Has 'The Organization Man' Aged?;
     Nostalgia's Illusions," *The New York Times*, January 17, 1999, http://www.
     nytimes.com/1999/01/17/opinion/dialogue-how-has-the-organization-man-
     aged-nostalgia-s-illusions.html.

MODULE 8
PLACE IN THE AUTHOR'S WORK

KEY POINTS

* Whyte remains one of the great American urban and social critics of the twentieth century.

* Whyte went on to have a distinguished career in urban theory and design stemming from his study of Park Forest, Ilinois in the USA.

* *The Organization Man* launched Whyte into the public and academic arena and its success fueled decades of continued notable work in urban development and academic research.

Positioning

The Organization Man was Whyte's first major book, building on several years of journalism and editorial work on similar subjects at *Fortune* magazine. The topics discussed in *The Organization Man* are the product of years of work in the field of business and management. Several of his early articles published at *Fortune* and other journals contributed to chapters or themes in *The Organization Man*, such as "The Wives of Management" (*Fortune*, 1951), "The Corporation and the Wife" (*Fortune*, 1951), "The Fallacies of Personal Testing" (*Fortune*, 1 954), "The Consumer in the New Suburbia" (Consumer Behavior, 1954), and "Budgetism: Opiate of the Middle Class" (*Fortune*, 1956), and his prior book critiquing business communication: *Is Anybody Listening?* published in 1952. Sponsorship by *Fortune* and private funding from Laurance Rockefeller allowed him to spend several years interviewing corporate executives and assembling his prior work and new findings into *The Organization Man*.[1]

> **" When William Whyte's *The Organization Man* came out in 1956, a powerful image of suburban life was seared into the public imagination. "**
> Becky Nicolaides and Andrew Wiese, *The Suburb Reader*

Even though *The Organization Man* was so successful, Whyte shifted his focus toward urban theory, design, and urbanization shortly after its completion, and went on to become an even more distinguished and well-published scholar in this field. After leaving *Fortune* in 1958, he worked as a Sociology Professor at Hunter College in New York City and rose to prominence with the title of Distinguished Professor.

Integration

It is possible to divide Whyte's work into two main categories. The first comprises the business articles and books published while working for *Fortune* Magazine, such as *Is Anybody Listening?* and *The Organization Man*. The second includes his subsequent work on urban design and urban planning seen in his later, but equally significant works, such as *The Last Landscape*, *The Social Life of Small Urban Spaces*, and the many pieces of urban critique for his research organization "The Project for Public Space."

Although there is a transition point in Whyte's career following the publication of *The Organization Man*, there is a consistent arc to his ideas and methods. Whyte's primary concern in *The Organization Man*, and in later urban works, was of people's lives and interactions. Whyte developed the technique of "Participant Observation" (also called Participant Observer Research), and continued to use this practical but original technique to understand how people interacted with one another and with the spaces they inhabited. While this connection between *The Organization Man* and Whyte's later work is a logical continuation, most critics separate this book from his later work on urban issues.

The Organization Man put Whyte on the map, and made him a household name. Whyte was ever so slightly ahead of the literary curve of mass-culture critiques, earning him a place at the front of the line among those who saw the detriments and trade-offs being willingly sacrificed for a society of conformity and reassurance. His work has been referenced, and parodied, dozens of times, with different sides of the argument claiming it to be either outdated or superbly relevant for subsequent generations.

Significance

The Organization Man is one of the most important business and management books ever written, and continues to be widely recognized as a classic and seminal text. However, after leaving *Fortune* magazine in 1958, Whyte changed directions and went on to develop a significant body of work in urban theory and social research, which is equally compelling and integral to modern scholarship.

Whyte continued to use the same methods of information-gathering that he had developed in his research for *The Organization Man* and these contributed to his original ideas on topics around public space use and urban development more broadly. Whyte, with continued backing from Laurance Rockefeller, went on to become a Professor at Hunter College in New York City and later developed the Project for Public Space, a research-based organization that employed some of these same research methods to urban space design. By the time Whyte had prepared books on urban space criticism, his success with *The Organization Man* helped promote him to bestseller status again in his "second career," while the financial gain from selling more than two million copies helped finance his later research.

Whyte's career can be summarized as the curious, thoughtful, and detailed exploration of the world around him, a world characterized by the notion that pleasant and willing conformity could provide men, and their families, with safety and stability.

NOTES

1   Michael Kaufman, "'Organization Man' Author and Urbanologist, Is Dead at 81," *The New York Times, January 13, 1999,* http://www.nytimes. com/1999/01/13/arts/william-h-whyte-organization-man-author-and-urbanologist-is-dead-at-81.html?pagewanted=all&src=pm.

SECTION 3
IMPACT

MODULE 9
THE FIRST RESPONSES

KEY POINTS

- Initial reactions to *The Organization Man* were largely positive, with many contemporary authors acknowledging its importance.

- *The Organization Man* launched a number of similar critiques on conformity,* suburbanization,* and mass culture.*

- Whyte shifted focus to urban design issues shortly after publication of *The Organization Man*.

Criticism

The Organization Man was wildly popular with both scholars and the general public, selling more than two million copies[1] and launching a host of other similar critiques on conformity within American culture. Whyte's work was quickly absorbed into a larger societal critique, which in some ways altered or masked his true intentions. "Whyte argued that corporate America was not entrepreneurial or risk-taking, as it fancied itself, but cautious and conformist. Whyte's *Organization Man* rapidly became confused with the hero of a popular novel, Sloan Wilson's* *The Man in the Gray Flannel Suit*."[2]

However, soon after publication, the world of *The Organization Man* began to quickly change, and this change in society attracted criticism of Whyte's work. "Peter Drucker* once remarked that no social theory was disproved so quickly as that of Organization Man. Far from ushering in an age of docile conformity, the 1960s and beyond saw an explosion of colorful individuality … Rock music did more to untie young people from their stifling suburban roots than

> ❝ With the rise of the postwar corporation, American individualism had disappeared from the mainstream of middle-class life. ❞
>
> Virginia Postrel, "Dialogue: How Has 'The Organization Man' Aged? Nostalgia's Illusions"

any revival of old-style Protestant Ethic ideology. Across huge swathes of society, throughout the free world, we saw the death of deference. I imagine Whyte would have cheered this on, but it is not what he predicted. It was certainly not a revolt of the Organization Men (or women – a group that Whyte, like virtually all his contemporaries, did not see coming). The Cultural Revolution came from their sons – and daughters."[3]

Responses

Whyte received much praise in book reviews and comments from fellow authors shortly after publication, many of which confirmed the trends he had observed and described and underscored their importance. "C. Wright Mills, whose own pioneering work, *The Power Elite* appeared in 1956, said of Mr. Whyte in The New York Times Book Review 'Crawling to the Top': 'He understands that the work-and-thrift ethic of success has grievously declined -- except in the rhetoric of top executives; that the entrepreneurial scramble to success has been largely replaced by the organizational crawl.'"[4]

In his own words, Whyte has stated that he was largely misunderstood. "Thirty years after 'The Organization Man' appeared, Mr. Whyte recalled how some of the people he had called organization men were angered by the designation. 'I meant no slight,' he said in 1986. 'Quite the contrary. My point was that these were the people who were running the country, not the rugged individualists of American folklore.'"[5]

"A pleasant, mild-mannered man given to tweed jackets at weekends, Whyte was upset to be classified as a social critic. He was surprised by the hostility of the business executives he had described with such understanding. 'They said I was calling them dirty conformists,' he lamented in 1986, 'but I wasn't. I was an organizational man myself.'"[6]

Other friendly critics cite Whyte's post-publication defense of his research as retaining great importance to his overall message to the public. "He bent over backward to prevent his famous book from being merely 'a censure of the fact of organization society,' and in an allusion to a popular novel of the day, Sloan Wilson's *The Man in the Gray Flannel Suit*, he wrote: 'Unless one believes poverty ennobling, it is difficult to see the three-button suit as more of a straitjacket than overalls, or the ranch-type house than old law tenements.'"[7]

Conflict and Consensus

Whyte spoke out about his incorrect critiques, attempting to shape the public's perception of his work. Whyte says himself: "This book is not a plea for nonconformity. Such pleas have an occasional therapeutic value, but as an abstraction, nonconformity is an empty goal, and rebellion against prevailing opinion merely because it is prevailing should no more be praised than acquiescence to it. Indeed, it is often a mask for cowardice, and few are more pathetic than those who flaunt outer differences to expiate their inner surrender ... there will be no strictures in this book against "Mass Man" ... nor will there be any strictures against ranch wagons, or television sets, or gray flannel suits ... the man who drives a Buick Special and lives in a ranch-type house just like hundreds of other ranch-type houses can assert himself as effectively and courageously against his particular society as the bohemian against his particular society ... the fault is not in organization, in short; it is in our worship of it."[8]

However, as the popularity of *The Organization Man* continued to grow, and Whyte moved on to other topics, Whyte's own statements about its meaning became lost in popular culture's interpretation of his work. It can be easy to misinterpret or selectively quote Whyte's *Organization Man* without full understanding of the nuanced motives that propelled Whyte to a household name and *The Organization Man* to a classic character of yesterday.

NOTES

1   Richard LeGates and Frederic Stout, eds. *The City Reader* (Abingdon, UK: Routledge, 2015), 4.

2   Godfrey Hodgson, "Secret Life of US Corporations," *The Guardian*, January 15, 1999, https://www.theguardian.com/news/1999/jan/15/guardianobituaries1.

3   Richard Koch, "The Rise & Fall Of Organization Man," *Huffington Post*, March 14, 2017, https://www.huffingtonpost.com/entry/the-rise-fall-of-organization-man_us_58c7ded1e4b0d06aa6580497.

4   Michael Kaufman, "'Organization Man' Author and Urbanologist, Is Dead at 81," *The New York Times*, January 13, 1999, http://www.nytimes.com/1999/01/13/arts/william-h-whyte-organization-man-author-and-urbanologist-is-dead-at-81.html?pagewanted=all&src=pm.

5   Kaufman, "Organization Man."

6   Hodgson, "Secret Life."

7   Jonathan Yardley, "William Whyte, Man Of The Mid-Century," *The Washington Post*, January 18, 1999, https://www.washingtonpost.com/archive/lifestyle/1999/01/18/william-whyte-man-of-the-mid-century/608a4308-4551-44b0-a17c-d0aa46f44792/?utm_term=.7c4a230619e8.

8   William H. Whyte, *The Organization Man* (New York: Simon and Schuster, 1956), 13.

MODULE 10
THE EVOLVING DEBATE

KEY POINTS

- *The Organization Man* changed the public's perception of Fortune 500 corporations and then men who filled their junior executive ranks.

- The portraits Whyte painted in *The Organization Man* served as a non-fiction example of theoretical and fictional characterizations of the time.

- *The Organization Man* generated much debate between its supportive and disobliging critics.

Uses and Problems

William Whyte passed away January 12, 1999 at the age of 81. His death prompted a significant revival of interest in his work and his analysis of the state of corporate conformism. Retrospective criticism of *The Organization Man* focuses more on Whyte's interpretation of business society and his predictions for the, than on critiques of the work itself. Postrel* (1999) notes somewhat ironically that "Whyte lived long enough to achieve a paradoxical fate for a social critic: the world he once criticized had become the good old days." But *Organization Man* critics have identified a shift toward entrepreneurship. At Harvard, Lorsch* said, students in the 1950s eagerly sought jobs with Fortune 500 companies. Today, "the better students don't want to go near them. They want to make money quickly in finance or venture capital or consulting or start-ups."[1]

Another change is that organizations, both corporate and public, no longer provide the lifetime employment security, pensions, and other benefits once assumed standard by the first generation of

> **❝** *The Organization Man* survives as a modern classic because it captures a permanent part of our social condition. **❞**
>
> Robert Samuelson, *Untruth: Why the Conventional Wisdom is (Almost Always) Wrong*

Organization Men. Whyte noted, "Be loyal to the company and the company will be loyal to you,"[2] but that is on longer the case. Companies have drastically cut middle management positions, benefits, and pensions, making it no longer nearly as attractive to sign onto a single organization for one's entire career.

Schools of Thought

Critics have noted the increased self-reliance of the more recent generations of employees and their need to fend for themselves, driven by both a bottom-up attitude shift and a top-down "employment at will" workforce. "Today's executive is more cynical about what America can do, more self-expressive and less willing to sacrifice his personal life for the good of the corporation. He may even quit the big company and start a new business using his experience or quit work altogether for a year of travel. That is the conclusion of management consultant Paul Leinberger,* who says the baby boom generation has translated the American work ethic into an 'enterprise ethic.'"[3]

Several scholars have explored this shift in perspective by examining the children of Organization Men described by Whyte, and how their experience of growing up in households headed by Organization Men has shaped their own perspectives on the workplace and their career goals. Many saw their fathers devote their lives unconditionally to the company, only to be shown little to no loyalty in return: "Having grown up in the 1950s and 1960s, their view of organizations is different," Leinberger told *Reuters** in an interview. "They saw how their fathers had been betrayed, how they had worked 60-70 hours a week, or had been moved across the country every few years without ever questioning it, only to be fired because of a corporate buyout, oil shock or restructuring."[4]

In Current Scholarship

Some critics note that Whyte's observations, while accurate, were perfunctory and straightforward, and note how different circumstances are today. As Whyte has stated: "For them society has in fact been good—very, very good—for there has been a succession of fairly beneficent environments: college, the paternalistic, if not always pleasant, military life, then, perhaps, graduate work through the G.I. Bill of Rights, a corporation apprenticeship during a period of industrial expansion and high prosperity … The system, they instinctively conclude, is beneficent."[5] In contrast, we see that this is not the case today. "Nowadays, of course, only a small percentage of Americans have military experience, colleges leave graduates with unpayable debt burdens, the economy keeps trying and so far failing to bust out of a post-crisis funk, and 18.8% of the population of Park Forest is below the poverty line. It is a very different, less beneficent era from the one Whyte described."[6]

Yet critics have found Whyte's work to be astutely accurate for the time. "For nearly half a century after the book appeared, the organization man typified the professional. In most parts of the world, huge corporations—private, public, and government-owned—employed hundreds of thousands of organization men … Endless movies idolized devoted company men in gray flannel suits and the stable life they enjoyed."[7]

In 1991, Paul Leinberger, the son of one of Whyte's original Organization Men, and Bruce Tucker published a follow-up companion to Whyte's work, titled *The New Individualists: The*

Generation After The Organization Man. The authors spent more than seven years conducting follow-up interviews with more than 300 children of Whyte's original Organization Men in an attempt to both characterize this subset of the Baby Boom generation as well as pick up on the profiling of Organization Men where Whyte left off.[8] "The authors ... purport to probe such issues as: how the life experiences of this minority segment of the 75-million-strong baby-boom generation compare with those of its parents; occupational rivalry; socioeconomic trends in a post-metropolitan era; and the widespread urge to be creative."[9]

NOTES

1   Sumantra Ghoshal, Christopher A. Bartlett, and Peter C. Kovner, *The individualized corporation* (Harper Audio, 1997).

2   William H. Whyte, *The Organization Man* (New York: Simon & Schuster, 1956) 129.

3   Reuters, "The Organization Man - Big Changes Since the '50s," *Los Angeles Times,* December 9, 1987, http:/articles.latimes.com/1987-12-09/business/fi-18477_1_organization-man).

4   Reuters, "Big Changes."

5   Whyte, *The Organization Man*, 320.

6   Justin Fox, "The Bedraggled Return of the Organization Man," *Harvard Business Review,* June 5, 2013.

7   Mohan Babu, "From Organization Man to Free Agent," *Computer,* Infosys Technologies Limited, 2004,http:/ieeexplore.ieee.org/stamp/stamp.jsp?arnumber=1319294.

8   Kirkus Review of *The New Individualists: The Generation After The Organization Man* by Paul Leinberger & Bruce Tucker, *Kirkus Review*, May 10, 2010, https:/www.kirkusreviews.com/book-reviews/paul-leinberger/the-new-individualists/.

9   Kirkus, Review of *The New Individualists.*

MODULE 11
IMPACT AND INFLUENCE TODAY

KEY POINTS

- *The Organization Man* remains a part of popular debate today in both business and urban planning literature.

- Many feel *The Organization Man* is a relevant, but dated, critique on workplace dynamics and employee motivation.

- While some critics see today's employee as a stark contrast to Whyte's Organization, others develop a more nuanced critique.

Position

Whyte's critics have yet to form a consensus not only of his book as a work of its time, but of its place in current-day culture. "Capitalism proved more dynamic, and far more creative, than Whyte expected."[1]

Whyte has been criticized because he assumed the shift from Protestant to Social Ethic was permanent. "The implicit premise of the book was that the change was permanent: that the Organization Man and all he represented would henceforth define the American character. That Whyte's conformist organization represented the mature form of capitalism was conventional wisdom until fairly recently. We lived, critics and supporters agreed, in what John Galbraith* called "the technostructure" … Technology and capital markets had made entrepreneurship, and unpredictable economic evolution, obsolete. At least that's what the wise men of the 50's, 60's and 70's believed."[2]

Peter Drucker, management consultant and author, agreed: "no social theory was disproved so quickly as that of The Organization Man."[3] Drucker made these observations in the context of personal

> **❝** The Organization Man, whom we first met in 1956, is still very much with us. **❞**
>
> Kevin Williamson, "Why Corporate Leaders Became Progressive Activists"

satisfaction associated with knowledge work, something Whyte made little comment on. Whyte did not much discuss the personal motivations of employment aside from financial security and overall stability within an organization. No doubt there were many trained engineers at these same large corporations who found personal enjoyment and fulfillment from the study of their core subjects and the invention and development of new, life-changing technologies such as space exploration equipment and personal computers.

Interaction

Today, an Organization Man is considered something of a knowing sell-out and a mindless loyalist, a "yes man" who takes direction with little question or pushback and who delights in not having to make many any hard decisions. He was at once everyone and nobody.

"*The Organization Man* reminds us how easily social critics can confuse passing cultural moments with permanent transformations. But it also provides an antidote to the nostalgia for postwar corporatism. The world we've lost wasn't all today's stability zealots make it seem. 'Loyalty' sounds good in the abstract, but it exacts a terrible cost in economic stagnation and personal repression."[4] We continue to see reference to Whyte's characterization in both serious academic work and in pop culture. In "The Organization Kid," (2001), *New York Times* columnist David Brooks described the (then) current generation of elite college students as behaving in similar ways to the Organization Men of their grandfather's generation: "The young men and women of America's future elite work their laptops to the bone, rarely question authority, and happily accept their positions at the top of the heap as part of the natural order of life."[5] The implication is that this generation of young adults has lost the ability to challenge authority, stand up for causes, or launch a protest–activities considered standard and requisite for their parents at a similar age.

The Continuing Debate

Several recent critics argue that Whyte was misunderstood and that the "scathing criticisms" were not criticisms at all, but in-depth, mostly objective accounts of the trends developing around him. Just as Whyte did, authors continue to seek insight into the generation-defining motivations and behaviors of the current workforce. In 1995, Rutgers University labor-studies professor Charles Heckscher* published *White-Collar Blues: Management Loyalties in an Age of Corporate Restructuring,* the review of which was published in the *Wall Street Journal* under the title "So Long, Organization Man." Virginia Postrel examined Heckscher's contribution to the modern Organization Man ethic: "Mr. Heckscher finds a new attitude ... the 'professional ethic.' The 'professionals' are motivated by loyalty to a particular task, a mission, not to the organization as an entity. They do not expect lifetime security, and they do expect to be rewarded for performance ... they stay until the mission is accomplished, and they seek not only financial reward but challenges."[6]

Other authors also note the sharp differences in characteristics of today's most successful current business men and women: "The well-rounded fellow who gets along with pretty much everyone and isn't overly brilliant at anything sees his status trading near an all-time low. And all those brilliant screwballs whose fate Whyte bemoaned are sitting now on top of corporate America."[7] However, these same authors that critique Whyte's work in the context of the present day still support his methods. "My premise is that Whyte's line of inquiry is still as valid as it ever was: The way people organize themselves to make money influences the way they do a lot of other things."[8]

"Forty years later the remarkable thing about Whyte's description of American business life is how thoroughly wrong it sounds. It may even have been wrong, or at least exaggerated, at the time. But the Organization Man, if he ever existed, is dead now."[9] However, it may be too soon to make this judgment. As Whyte reminds us, "… what may be abnormal today is very likely to be normal tomorrow."[10]

NOTES

1 Virginia Postrel, "Dialogue: How Has 'The Organization Man' Aged?; Nostalgia's Illusions," *The New York Times*, January 17, 1999, http://www. nytimes.com/1999/01/17/opinion/dialogue-how-has-the-organization-man-aged-nostalgia-s-illusions.html.

2 Postrel, "Dialogue."

3 Peter Drucker, "The Age of Social Transformation," *The Atlantic Monthly*, November 1994, https://www.theatlantic.com/past/docs/politics/ecbig/ soctrans.htm.

4 Postrel, "Dialogue."

5 David Brooks, "The Organization Kid," *The Atlantic*, April 2001, https://www. theatlantic.com/magazine/archive/2001/04/the-organization-kid/302164/.

6 Postrel, "Dialogue."

7 Michael Lewis, "The New Organization Man," *Slate magazine, October 30, 1997,* http://www.slate.com/articles/arts/millionerds/1997/10/the_new_ organization_man.html.

8 Lewis, "The New Organization Man."

9 Lewis, "The New Organization Man."

10 William H. Whyte, The Organization Man (New York: Simon & Schuster, 1956), 267.

WHERE NEXT?

KEY POINTS

- Changes in workforce characteristics have discredited many of Whyte's arguments for today's professional.
- Whyte's work will remain a critical piece of business and social history, as it evaluates the employee's relationship with his employer and with his line of work.
- *The Organization Man* defined a term, a typology, and a generation, and has become a part of our cultural history.

Potential

The Organization Man captures an enduring question in a specific moment in time, a moment that both has a certain nostalgia and that we see as backward, outdated, and discriminatory according to our current perspective. The publication of the most recent edition ensures the text will remain readily available for the next generation of readers, while the term in colloquial speech will continue to appear in everyday references.

"Of course, it all sounds like nonsense today. Now we associate technology with change, not predictability. Corporations cherish flexibility, leanness and just-in-time management. 'Creative destruction' is the rule. Men–and, this time around, women–of ambition seek their *Fortunes* not in bureaucratic conformity but in adaptability, entrepreneurship and job-hopping."[1]

The Organization Man will likely always remain a classic, although as it ages it will perhaps be misinterpreted more often as it becomes detached from its context. Today's workforce is harder to categorize, generalize, and stereotype, making it difficult to imagine a new version

> ❝ Whyte's ethnography now looks socially obsolete
> ... The stability of life-long commitment to the
> company has collapsed in the face of intense economic
> competition in a global economy. ❞
>
> Bryan S. Turner, *International Encyclopedia of the Social Sciences*

of Whyte's sweeping classic taking such a widespread hold. We see a
deluge of articles and critiques on today's generation of young
employees and the millennial workforce, but the academic and
professional tone is more of a conversation than a single top-down
characterization.

Future Directions

"This cultural and economic dynamism deeply troubles today's social
critics, who seem to prefer stasis," writes Virginia Postrel. "On the
right, Pat Buchanan* longs for 'the kind of social stability, rootedness
... we all used to know,' the world in which his father lived in the same
place and worked at the same job his whole life. On the left, the
sociologist Richard Sennett* writes a book on the 'new capitalism'
called *The Corrosion of Character*. The old hierarchies, he argues, gave
people a sense of purpose and control, a linear narrative of their lives.
Without that, he suggests, 'the corroding of character is an inevitable
consequence.' Though some might deny it, such critics want to bring
back the Organization Man and the orderly, predictable world in
which he lived. In economic and social diversity, they see only
fragmentation. In business innovation, they discern only disorder. In
the fading of 'belongingness,' they imagine the death of character."[2]

Ethnographic scholars continue to use Whyte's methods of
participant observation to explore a wide range of issues related to
both workplace culture and urban/suburban development and
function. Whyte's death in 1999 saw a resurgence of interest in his

work, with some scholars seeking to characterize the next generation of Organization Men. However, as the collective memory of the public becomes focused on new business challenges, Whyte's *The Organization Man* will probably fade from the contemporary business field. Its historical significance, though, will no doubt keep it relevant as a generation-defining characterization of both employee and family man.

Contemporary critics remind us not to allow nostalgia for the world of the Organization Man to cloud our collective memory of reality. "In 2014, the world looks vastly different. In many ways, it's better. Racism and sexism aren't gone, by any stretch, but they've subsided in concrete ways: for example, now it's not weird for men to have female bosses. The globalization that threatens certain kinds of mid-century middle-class jobs also reflects the basic fact that billions of people aren't sentenced to labor camps for bad-mouthing the Chairman anymore. The kind of confident sexism for which the CU-Boulder philosophy department has been nationally shamed was once—and not all that long ago—utterly normal. It still exists, but now it's considered aberrant. That's a form of progress, however imperfect."[3]

Summary
The Organization Man has become much more than a book title, it has entered our colloquial language and in some ways defined, at least stereo-typically, a generation. The *Oxford English Dictionary* even lists it as an official term: (noun) A man who lets his individuality and personal life be dominated by the organization he serves.[4]

The Organization Man will likely forever remain a fixture of American midcentury culture, one that scholars, critics, and mass media will continue to revisit. For example, the widely popular American television series *Mad Men* has prompted several essays comparing the lead character, Donald Draper, to an Organization Man.[5] Yet the relationship we have with our occupation, place of employment, and the tradeoffs we make in order to provide for our families will always be topics of intense debate and discussion. Whyte showed us one way of researching, exploring, and characterizing how we navigate the work–life balance. He provided, too, the foundation for current scholarship and commentary on a wide range of interrelated topics that circle around these core themes.

The world has changed drastically since Whyte introduced us to *The Organization Man.* The impact of technology, globalization, fiscal and international policy, diversity, and family dynamics have all, in multiple ways, negated the environment that produced *The Organization Man.* Whyte's work has remained a controversial conversation starter for more than 50 years, and is still vivid in our collective memory, where it will likely remain for generations.

NOTES

1   Virginia Postrel, "Dialogue: How Has 'The Organization Man' Aged?; Nostalgia's Illusions," *The New York Times, January 17, 1999,* http://www. nytimes.com/1999/01/17/opinion/dialogue-how-has-the-organization-man-aged-nostalgia-s-illusions.html.

2   Postrel, "Dialogue."

3   Matt Reed, "Anyone Remember the Organization Man?" Inside Higher Ed, February 4, 2014, https://www.insidehighered.com/blogs/confessions-community-college-dean/anyone-remember-organization-man.

4   Oxford English Dictionary. https://en.oxforddictionaries.com/definition/ organization_man.

5   Bob Greene, "A Lesson On What`s Inside The Suit," *The Chicago Tribune, January 8, 1992.* http://articles.chicagotribune.com/1992-01-08/ features/9201020859_1_executive-suite-rich-magazine-story.

GLOSSARY

GLOSSARY OF TERMS

1984 (Nineteen Eighty-Four): a classic novel published in 1949 by English author George Orwell. He describes a future dystopian society that requires overwhelming conformism and monitors the thoughts of its citizens by a "Thought Police."

Aptitude Test: a test designed to assess a subject's ability or proficiency in one or more given subject or technological area.

Army Alpha Test: a group-administered test given by the United States military to evaluate the intellectual and emotional capabilities of new army recruits during World War I.

Baby Boom (generation): the generation of Americans born between roughly 1945 and 1964 (approximately 65 million births). They are generally considered to have grown up in the prosperity and economic security of the 1950s before beginning to sharply question authority in the mid-1960s in periods of social and political turmoil related to the Civil Rights Movement and the Vietnam War.

Bell Labs: major American technological research and development lab, named after Alexander Graham Bell, one of the inventors of the telephone. It is currently owned by Finnish telecommunications company Nokia and headquartered in New Jersey.

Benjamin Franklin Maxims: wisdom quotations and adages published by Franklin in *Poor Richard's Almanac* from 1732 to 1757. The most popular ones include "Well done is better than well said," and "Haste makes waste."

Bernreuter Personality Inventory: a personality test developed by American psychologist Robert Bernreuter in 1931 and one of the most popular tests in the 1930s.

Bourgeoisie: French term that is commonly used to refer to the middle class. In a Marxist context it refers to the capitalist class that owns and manages the capital (wealth) and means of production in society.

Budgetism: a household budgeting practice that often involved borrowing money and taking on debt in order to buy a house, car or other possessions, rather than saving for these purchases and paying cash.

The Caine Mutiny: (novel, 1951; film, 1954) an American film based on the novel by Herman Wouk. It tells the fictional story of the US Navy stationed in the Pacific during World War II and the moral dilemma of challenging authority to the point of mutiny to protect safety and security of fellow crewmembers. Wouk was awarded the Pulitzer Prize for the novel and the film received numerous Oscar nominations. Both film and novel were widely popular.

Capitalism: an economic theory based on private ownership, markets, and free enterprise.

Cold War (1947–1991): a period of high global tension between the Soviet Union and western countries that ended with the fall of the Soviet Union in 1991.

Collectivism: the ideology or philosophy that emphasizes the community or group above the individual.

Conformity: acting in accord with generally accepted social standards and rules.

Consumerism: social and economic circumstances that encourage the consumption of goods and services.

Executive Suite: an American film released in 1954 that tells the story of a furniture manufacturing company after the CEO has passed away and the ruthless struggle for company control by other employees.

Fortune **magazine:** a multi-national business magazine published by Time Inc. and founded by Henry Luce in 1929.

Fourier Settlements: American utopian communities based on the principles of utopian socialism developed by French philosopher Charles Fourier.

Frankfurt School (Frankfurter Schule): a school of philosophy and social theory founded in the early twentieth century and based within the Institute for Social Research at Goethe University in Frankfurt, Germany. Frankfurt School scholars developed texts on Critical Theory, Capitalism, Social Theory, and Popular Culture. Notable scholars included Max Weber and Jürgen Habermas.

French Revolution (1789–1799): a period of turmoil in France during which the monarchy was overthrown. Though it began with the espousal of liberal political and social ideas, it ended with the establishment of a dictatorship under Napoleon. It triggered a number of related global conflicts and had far-reaching impacts on global economics, religion, and politics.

From Here to Eternity: (novel, 1951, film, 1953) a popular American film released in 1953 based on the 1951 novel by James Jones of the same name. It is the story of Robert E. Lee Prewitt, a soldier in Hawaii in 1941, who is criticized for refusing to showcase his boxing skills in the wake of a love affair.

"GI" (Government Issue, General Issue): term originally used to refer to military equipment made of "galvanized iron" during WWII, but as the war progressed its meaning morphed into "general issue," indicating war supplies issued to soldiers and then "government issue," ultimately referring to the soldiers themselves. The popular action figure "GI Joe" was named after World War II GIs.

GI Bill (Servicemen's Readjustment Act of 1944): American legislation designed to provide benefits to soldiers returning home from World War II service. These included low-cost home mortgages, college tuition assistance, and unemployment compensation. The benefits provided had a significant impact on launching the strong economy enjoyed by Americans in the 1950s and supported the growth of the "baby boom" generation.

Gemutlichkeit: a German term used in the English language to indicate a feeling of warmth and friendliness.

General Education: refers to common or general coursework that forms the foundation of post-secondary (university) education in the United States.

God and Man at Yale: The Superstitions of "Academic Freedom": a book published in 1951 by William Buckley, Jr. that claimed that Yale University was robbing students of their freedom by forcing them to adopt the liberal ideals of collectivism and secularization.

The book was based on Buckley's experiences as an undergraduate student at Yale.

Group Dynamics: a psychological and social topic evaluation of human behaviors and processes within or between social groups.

Great Depression (1929–1941): a period in United States history characterized by significant economic depression, lack of employment, and a significant decrease in overall gross domestic product. The Great Depression originated in the United States but impacted the global economy.

Great Recession: period of economic decline related to the bursting of the 'housing bubble' in the United States in 2008.

Guggenheim Foundation (Solomon R. Guggenheim Foundation): an American nonprofit foundation "dedicated to promoting the understanding and appreciation of art, primarily of the modern and contemporary periods, through exhibitions, education programs, research initiatives, and publications."

Harwald Group Thinkometer: a mechanical polling device to aid in group brainstorming by allowing members to press buttons to indicate yes, no, or maybe, thus allowing members to poll opinions without revealing their identity.

High Noon: an American western film released in 1952 that tells the fictional story of a law officer who must choose between his duty to the safety of his town and love for his new wife in the face of gang violence. The popular film won four Academy Awards and is included in the United States Film Registry as part of the Library of Congress.

Horatio Alger Myth: an American fictional "rags to riches" story that shows a protagonist being rewarded with great financial success and fame after overcoming challenges with hard work and dedication. Author Horatio Alger published more than 100 such novels that embody the Protestant Ethic of hard work and thrift as key to one's self-determined success in the second half of the nineteenth century.

Industrial Revolution (1760–1840): a period of technological transition to modern industrial equipment and processes.

Kaffeeklatsch: a German term used to mean chitchat or gossip at an informal gathering, usually in one's home, and often where coffee is served.

"Keeping up with the Joneses": a popular American colloquial phrase that refers to social and peer pressure to maintain a home and lifestyle similar to one's neighbors. The phrase originated from the early twentieth-century comic strip of the same name which portrayed the McGinis family and their efforts to "keep up" with their neighbors, the Jones family.

Kibbutz: Israeli/Hebrew term for a collective, agricultural cooperative in Israel.

Labor Theories: a body of literature focused on labor organization, labor dynamics, and labor/workforce management.

Labor Union: an organization designed to unite and protect works of a given trade and location by advocating for the advancement of wage, rights, benefits, and working conditions.

The Lamp: Company periodical journal and employee magazine published by the Standard Oil Company (later Jersey Standard).

League of Women Voters: American civic organization founded during the suffrage movement in 1920. It continues to remain an active civic organization promoting democratic and progressive causes, such as universal health care, abortion rights, and campaign finance reform.

Levittown: any of the seven large suburban housing developments constructed by Levitt & Sons in the 1950s and 1960s, located in New York, New Jersey, Maryland, Pennsylvania, and Puerto Rico. These developments were primarily occupied by returning World War II veterans and have been heavily criticized for their uniformity, homogeneity, and lack of racial diversity. The name is synonymous with suburban sprawl.

Mass Culture: (also popular, or pop culture) the set of cultural ideas and viewpoints that arise from a common cultural experience or a common exposure to media, news, music, and art.

Man in the Grey Flannel Suit: (book by Sloan Wilson, 1955; film released in 1956) the fictional story of an American businessman who debates the pros and cons of corporate success and financial gain in contrast with family time and values. Both the book and film were wildly popular, and considered by many to be the fictionalization of Whyte's Organization Man. They became a cultural emblem for 1950s post-war America.

A Man Called Peter: a popular 1955 American film based on the life of religious leader Peter Marshall.

Management Literature: body of literature focused on business-related topics, such as management, strategy, organizational dynamics, talent planning, and innovation.

Marxism: the political and economic theories of Karl Marx and Friedrich Engels that form the basis of Communism.

New Deal (1933–1937): a group of economic stimulus programs launched by President Franklin D. Roosevelt to help mitigate the impacts of the Great Depression and spur economic recovery for the United States which focused on the "Three Rs: Relief, Recovery, and Reform." Some of the most popular New Deal programs included the Works Progress Administration, the Tennessee Valley Authority, the Federal Deposit Insurance Corporation, and the Federal Housing Authority.

New Thought Movement: a philosophical movement in nineteenth century America that focused on the infinite and supreme nature of God and the notion that the mental state of a person is translated into daily life. It is based on the teachings of Phineas Quimby and shares some overlap with the principles of Christian Scientists.

Oneida Community: a religious-based perfectionist community located in Oneida, New York, USA founded in 1848 by John Noyes. It was disbanded in 1881.

Organizational Dynamics: the process an organization uses to foster organizational learning and strategic management; the process of strengthening resources and employee performance.

The Origins of American Scientists: article published in Science (1951) by Robert Knapp and Hubert Goodrich describing and cataloging the academic backgrounds of American scientists.

Package Suburb: a term referring to the new suburbs developed in the 1950s in the United States that provided a "full package" of amenities, such as the Levittowns in New York, New Jersey, and Pennsylvania, and Park Forest, Illinois.

Park Forest, Illinois: a middle-class suburb of Chicago developed in 1948 as a planned, self-governed community.

Personality Test: a type of psychological test (of which there are many variations) designed to help identify personality, management, style, and cultural fit for employees or recruits. Popular current examples include the Myers–Briggs Type Indicator, which is commonly used in corporate and government bureaucracies.

The Philosophy of Labor: a book published by Frank Tannenbaum in 1951 that discusses the importance of labor unions in society and community.

'Post-World War II' Period: the period of prosperity and strong economic growth beginning after the end of the second world war in 1945 and ending with the recession of 1973-1975. Benefits were primarily concentrated in the United States, Western Europe, and East Asia.

Revolving Credit: a line of credit for consumers where the credit is automatically renewed as debts are paid down, popular for department store purchases.

Rorschach Inkblot Test: a psychological test designed by Swiss psychologist Herman Rorschach in 1921.The test can be used on subjects from the aged 5 of five through to adulthood and is still widely used in many countries for identifying psychological and thought disorders as well as general predictive personality testing.

Scientism: the philosophical notion or practice of ascribing scientific theory and testing to other scientific or non-scientific areas of scholarship that are not appropriate for that domain.

The Sane Society: a book published by Erich Fromm in 1955 that critiques modern social and political philosophies.

Stanley Home Products/Party: American home keeping and housewares company that sold products through social gatherings led by local representatives in their homes, similar to a 'Tupperware' party. The company was founded in Massachusetts, USA in 1931 and remains in business, selling primarily home cleaning products.

Suburbanization: population and development shift from central urban areas to suburban areas, often resulting in suburban sprawl.

Thematic Apperception Test: a popular projective picture-based psychological test designed by Henry Murray and Christina Morgan in the 1930s and is still used today for assessing research subjects, criminals, and patients with various conditions.

Utopia/Utopian: an idealized or imagined community based on egalitarian principles.

Urban Theory and Design: a hybrid topic that draws upon sociology, economics, planning, and design to develop primarily democratic (leftist), post World War II ideas about city design, functionality, idealized and future development.

Urbanist: an advocate, scholar, or expert in urban issues and city planning.

VA (Veteran's Administration) Loan Program: home mortgage assistance program in the United States designed to help military service men and women purchase homes with little to no down payment and with reduced mortgage interest rates. The VA Loan Program was originally part of the GI Bill of 1944.

Vietnam War (1955-1975): the second colonial war between North and South Vietnam. The United States was heavily involved in fighting to prevent a communist takeover of South Vietnam. The war had high death tolls and was heavily protested.

Vick School of Applied Merchandising: the college recruiting and training program at the Vick Chemical Company designed to help new employees learn about the products and techniques for selling them to local and regional retailers.

Watergate Scandal: the 1972 political scandal in the United States under the Nixon Administration involving the burglary at the Democratic National Committee headquarters located in the Watergate Office Complex in Washington, DC. Then-President Richard Nixon attempted to cover up their involvement in the scandal, which led to Nixon's resignation.

Woman's World: an American film released in 1954 that tells the story of competition among employees at a large corporation.

World War II: (also called the Second World War) the largest and most deadly global conflict in history, occurring between 1939–1945. Two major military alliances developed: the Axis (Germany, Japan, and Italy) and Allied (USA, Soviet Union, United Kingdom, China) powers. The war ended when the Japanese surrendered on September 2, 1945.

Worthington Personal History: a personal history questionnaire used in employee recruiting and hiring.

PEOPLE MENTIONED IN THE TEXT

Adorno, Theodor (1903–1969) was a German sociologist and philosopher who was part of the Frankfurt School and best known for his work on Critical Theory of Society.

Jenny Bell Bechtel (1926–2002) was an American fashion designer and wife of William H. Whyte.

Walter Benjamin (1892–1940) was a German Philosopher best known for his work on Western Marxism. Walter collaborated with Max Horkheimer at the Institute for Social Research, part of the Frankfurt School.

Amanda Bennett (b. 1952) is an American journalist who worked for the *Wall Street Journal* for more than 20 years.

Archibald Allan Bowman (1893–1936) was a Scottish philosopher and Princeton University Professor whose work focused on the philosophy of religion.

Patrick Buchanan (b, 1938) is an American political commentator and author with a conservative focus.

Mark Carnes (b. 1950) is an American author who published *The Columbia History of Post-World War II America* in 2007.

Wallace Hume Carothers (1896–1937) was an American chemist and inventor who developed nylon while working for the DuPont Chemical Company.

John Dalton (1766–1884) was an English meteorologist, physicist, and scientist who proposed the modern atomic theory, which later enabled the creation of the Atomic Bomb.

Reuel Denney (1913–1995) was an American poet, professor and author who explored American popular culture. His most popular work is *The Astonished Muse*, published in 1957.

John Dewey (1859–1952) was an American scholar and proponent of Pragmatism, the idea that theories should be developed thorough hypothesis testing and experimentation rather than from passively observing the environment.

Peter Drucker (1909–2005) was a prominent management consultant and author whose work focused on human organization within management and management education.

Dwight D. Eisenhower (1890–1969) was the 34th President of the United States who served two terms in office, from 1953 to 1961.

Erich Fromm (1900–1980) was a German socialist and psychologist whose work focused on Critical Theory at the Frankfurt School. He went on to found the William Allison White Institute of Psychiatry in New York City.

John Kenneth Galbraith (1908–2006) was a Canadian economist and leading advocate of twentieth-century liberalism in America.

Charles Heckscher (b. 1949) is an American professor at Rutgers University who focuses on labor studies and employment. He published *White-Collar Blues: Management Loyalties in an Age of Corporate Restructuring* in 1995.

Max Horkheimer (1895–1978) was a German psychologist and sociologist whose work focused on Critical Theory at the Frankfurt School.

Jane Jacobs (1916–2006) was an American-Canadian scholar and author who wrote several classic books on urban planning principles, most notably *The Death and Life of Great American Cities*, published in 1961.

Philip Klutznick (1907–1999) was a United States Secretary of Commerce, large real estate developer, Jewish leader, and philanthropist who also served as the Commissioner of the Federal Public Housing Authority and later led the Urban Investment and Development Company.

Paul Leinberger (b, 1947) is an American author who published *The New Individualists: The Generation After the Organization Man* in 1991.

Jay Lorsch (b. 1932) is an American professor at the Harvard Business School who focuses on human resources and organizational theory.

Joseph Nocera (b. 1952) is an American journalist who is a business columnist for the *New York Times* and wrote for *Fortune* magazine for more than ten years.

Virginia Postrel (b. 1960) is an American political writer and critic known for her classically liberal viewpoints.

David Riesman (1909–2002) was an American sociologist and author who published *The Lonely Crowd: A Study of Changing American Character*, in 1950, an extremely popular book that critiqued the changing social and cultural circumstances in America.

Anne Roe (1909–1991) was an American clinical psychologist whose work focused on occupational psychology, and in particular, on people of high intellect. She published *The Making of a Scientist* in 1953.

Jean-Jacques Rousseau (1712–1778) was a French philosopher of the Enlightenment and French Revolutionary period who focused on the idea of the education of the whole person as requisite for citizenship and civic participation.

Richard Sennett (b. 1943) is an American professor at the London School of Economics and New York University who focuses on sociology in urban contexts.

Dr. Ruth Strang (1895–1971) was an American psychologist whose work focused on child and adolescent psychology. Her books on the subject were published widely and she was a Professor at the Teacher's College, part of Columbia University, In New York City.

Frank Tannenbaum (1893–1969) was an Austrian-American historian, sociologist, and scholar whose work focused on labor and trade and published widely on the subject. He was also a Professor of Latin American History at Columbia University in New York City.

Max Weber (1846–1920) was a German sociologist who developed important theories on workforce labor and economic theory. He published *The Protestant Ethic and the Spirit of Capitalism*, his most well known book, in 1905.

Alfred North Whitehead (1861–1947) was an English mathematician and philosopher who published *Principia Mathematica* in 1913, considered to be one of the most important contributions to mathematical logic in the twentieth century.

Frank Whittle (1907–1996) was an English aircraft engineer who is credited with developing the first operational jet engine.

William Foote Whyte (1914–2000) was an American sociologist and scholar whose research utilized participant observation techniques to understand inner city gangs in Boston and social interactions among urban residents. His primary work was *Street Corner Society*, published in 1943.

Sloan Wilson (1920–2003) was an American writer who published the novel *The Man in the Gray Flannel Suit* in 1955.

WORKS CITED

WORKS CITED

Adler, M. "Colleges Want to Cool Admissions Frenzy." National Public Radio, February 22, 2007. Accessed September 3, 2017.. http://www.npr.org/templates/story/story.php?storyId=7383744.

Archer, John. "Everyday Suburbia: Lives and Practices," Public: Art Culture Ideas. 43 (2011), 21-30.

Babu, Mohan. "From Organization Man to Free Agent." *Computer.* Infosys Technologies Limited, 2004. Accessed September 5, 2017. http://ieeexplore.ieee.org/stamp/stamp.jsp?arnumber=1319294.

Bennett, Amanda. *The Death of the Organization Man.* New York: William Morrow & Company, 1990.

Brooks, David. "The Organization Kid." *The Atlantic.* April 2001. Accessed August 2, 2017. https://www.theatlantic.com/magazine/archive/2001/04/the-organization-kid/302164/

Carnes, M. C. (Ed.). *The Columbia History of Post-World War II America.* New York: Columbia University Press, 2012.

Cohn, David. "Ballyhoo And Faith; IS ANYBODY LISTENING? How and Why U. S. Business Fumbles When It Talks With Human Beings," *The New York Times*, April 6, 1952.

Creadick, Anna G. *Perfectly average: The pursuit of normality in postwar America.* Amherst, MA: University of Massachusetts Press, 2010.

Drucker, Peter. "The Age of Social Transformation." *The Atlantic Monthly*, November 1994. Accessed September 3, 2017 .https://www.theatlantic.com/past/docs/politics/ecbig/soctrans.htm.

Fox, Justin. "The Bedraggled Return of the Organization Man." *Harvard Business Review.* June 5, 2013.

Ghoshal, Sumantra, Christopher A. Bartlett, and Peter C. Kovner. *The Individualized Corporation.* Harper Audio, 1997.

Groves, Martha. "Lessons From 'The Organization Man' Still Have Some Relevance for Today." *LA Times*, January 24, 1999. Accessed September 2, 2017. http://articles.latimes.com/1999/jan/24/business/fi-1115

Greene, Bob. "A Lesson On What`s Inside The Suit." *The Chicago Tribune*, January 8, 1992. Accessed October 2, 2017. http://articles.chicagotribune.com/1992-01-08/features/9201020859_1_executive-suite-rich-magazine-story.

Hodgson, Godfrey. "Secret Life of US Corporations." *Guardian*, January 15, 1999. Accessed August 4, 2017. https://www.theguardian.com/news/1999/jan/15/guardianobituaries1.

IBM. "The way we wore: A century of IBM attire" IBM Archives, Accessed October 2,2017. https://www03.ibm.com/ibm/history/exhibits/waywewore/waywewore_1.html.

"Jenny Bechtel Whyte, Fashion Designer, 75." *The New York Times*. September 4, 2002. Accessed October 30, 2017. http://www.nytimes.com/2002/09/04/nyregion/jenny-bechtel-whyte-fashion-designer-75.html.

Kaufman, Michael T. "'Organization Man' Author and Urbanologist, Is Dead at 81." *The New York Times*, January 13, 1999. Accessed August 2, 2017. http://www.nytimes.com/1999/01/13/arts/william-h-whyte-organization-man-author-and-urbanologist-is-dead-at-81.html?pagewanted=all&src=pm.

Kirkus. Review of *The New Individualists: The Generation After The Organization Man* by Paul Leinberger & Bruce Tucker. *Kirkus Review*, May 10, 2010, https://www.kirkusreviews.com/book-reviews/paul-leinberger/the-new-individualists/.

Koch, Richard. "The Rise & Fall Of Organization Man." *Huffington Post*. March 14, 2017. Accessed September 28, 2017. https://www.huffingtonpost.com/entry/the-rise-fall-of-organization-man_us_58c7ded1e4b0d06aa6580497.

Lafarge, Albert, ed. *The essential William H. Whyte*. New York: Fordham University Press, 2000.

Lawrence, Paul R. The *Changing of Organizational Behavior Patterns: A Case Study of Decentralization*. New Brunswick: Transaction publishers, 1958.

LeGates, Richard T., and Frederic Stout, eds. *The City Reader*. Abingdon: Routledge, 2015.

Levy, Claudia. "William Whyte Dies." *The Washington Post*, January 14, 1999. Accessed August 2, 2017. https://www.washingtonpost.com/archive/local/1999/01/14/william-whyte-dies/60436392-1f58-4fa3-a61a-1a6277d626bf/?utm_term=.111ccfc66f23.

Lewis, Michael. "The New Organization Man." *Slate* magazine, October 30, 1997. Accessed August 4, 2017. http://www.slate.com/articles/arts/millionerds/1997/10/the_new_organization_man.html.

Leonard, David. "William Whyte's The Organization Man." *Bloomberg*, December 4, 2014. https://www.bloomberg.com/news/articles/2014-12-04/the-organization-man-conformity-of-corporate-culture-revealed.

Mills, C. Wright. "Crawling to the Top," review of *The Organization Man* by William H. Whyte. *The New York Times*. December 9, 1956. Accessed October 2, 2017. http://www.nytimes.com/1956/12/09/archives/crawling-to-the-top-crawling-to-the-top.html.

Miller, Roger K. "'Organization Man' still a worthwhile read." Pittsburgh Tribune. June 11, 2016. Accessed September 28, 2017. http://triblive.com/x/pittsburghtrib/ae/books/s_456697.html.

Nicolaides, Becky M., and Andrew Wiese. *The Suburb Reader*. New York: Taylor & Francis, 2006.

Nocera, Joseph. Foreword to *The Organization Man*. Philadelphia: University of Pennsylvania Press, 2013.

Patterson, James. Grand Expectations: The United States, 1945-1974. New York: Oxford University Press, 1996, 312-317.

Pells, Richard H. *The liberal mind in a conservative age: American intellectuals in the 1940s and 1950s*. Middleton, CT: Wesleyan University Press, 1989.

Pollard, Garland. "Re-reading William Whyte's The Organization Man." *Garland Pollard Blog*. April 23, 2016. Accessed August 3, 2017. http://www.garlandpollard.com/re-reading-william-whytes-the-organization-man/

Postrel, Virginia. "Dialogue: How Has 'The Organization Man' Aged? Nostalgia's Illusions." *The New York Times*, January 17, 1999. Accessed August 3, 2017. http://www.nytimes.com/1999/01/17/opinion/dialogue-how-has-the-organization-man-aged-nostalgia-s-illusions.html.

Randall, Donna. "Commitment and the Organization: The Organization Man Revisited." *Academy of Management Review*, 1987, Vol. 12, No. 3, 460-471.

http://www.jstor.org/stable/pdf/258513.pdf?refreqid=excelsior%3A0a9742fe94fd6bf26211c59cc6f15745.

Rao, Venkatesh. "The Ideology of the Organization Man." *Ribbonfarm*. November 23, 2008. Accessed October 2, 2017. https://www.ribbonfarm.com/2008/11/23/the-ideology-of-the-organization-man/.

Reed, Matt. "Anyone Remember the Organization Man?"

Inside Higher Ed. February 4, 2014. Accessed September 28, 2017. https://www.insidehighered.com/blogs/confessions-community-college-dean/anyone-remember-organization-man.

Reuters. "The Organization Man – Big Changes Since the '50s." *Los Angeles Times,* December 9, 1987. Accessed September 2, 2017. http://articles.latimes.com/1987-12-09/business/fi-18477_1_organization-man.

Samuelson, Robert J. *Untruth: Why the Conventional Wisdom is (Almost Always) Wrong.* AtRandom, 2001.

Schee, Kris. "A Generation of Tools?" *MIT TECH*, October 16, 2001. Accessed September 15, 2017. http://tech.mit.edu/V121/N51/col51kris.51c.html.

Scott, William G., and David K. Hart. *Organizational Values in America.* Transaction Publishers, 1989.

Sernovitz, Gary. "What 'The Organization Man' Can Tell Us About Inequality Today." *The New Yorker.* December 29, 2016. Accessed August 2, 2017. http://www.newyorker.com/business/currency/what-the-organization-man-can-tell-us-about-inequality-today

Simon, Scott. "William Whyte: Ensuring That Cities Give People a 'Place for Dreams'." *Los Angeles Times.* July 22, 1990. Accessed August 2, 2017. http://articles.latimes.com/1990-07-22/opinion/op-639_1_american-cities.

Turner, Bryan S. "Organization Man," *International Encyclopedia of the Social Sciences,* 2008. Accessed August 2, 2017. http://www.encyclopedia.com/social-sciences-and-law/sociology-and-social-reform/sociology-general-terms-and-concepts-67.

Weber, Max. *The Protestant Ethic and the Spirit of Capitalism.* Trans. and ed. Peter Baehr and Gordon C. Wells. New York: Penguin, 2002 [1905].

Whyte, William H. "The Transients." *Fortune,* May 1953. Accessed September 15, 2017. http://Fortune.com/2015/12/25/the-transients-william-whyte-Fortune-1953/.

1956. *The Organization Man.* New York: Simon and Schuster.

Williamson, Kevin. "Why Corporate Leaders Became Progressive Activists." *National Review,* March 13, 2017. Accessed August 14, 2017, http://www.nationalreview.com/article/445705/corporate-leaders-progressive-activists-not-conservative-villains.

Yardley, Jonathan. "William Whyte, Man Of The Mid-Century." *The Washington Post,* January 18, 1999. Accessed August 2, 2017. https://www.washingtonpost.com/archive/lifestyle/1999/01/18/william-whyte-man-of-the-mid-century/608a4308-4551-44b0-a17c-d0aa46f44792/?utm_term=.7c4a230619e8.

THE MACAT LIBRARY
BY DISCIPLINE

AFRICANA STUDIES

Chinua Achebe's *An Image of Africa: Racism in Conrad's Heart of Darkness*
W. E. B. Du Bois's *The Souls of Black Folk*
Zora Neale Huston's *Characteristics of Negro Expression*
Martin Luther King Jr's *Why We Can't Wait*
Toni Morrison's *Playing in the Dark: Whiteness in the American Literary Imagination*

ANTHROPOLOGY

Arjun Appadurai's *Modernity at Large: Cultural Dimensions of Globalisation*
Philippe Ariès's *Centuries of Childhood*
Franz Boas's *Race, Language and Culture*
Kim Chan & Renée Mauborgne's *Blue Ocean Strategy*
Jared Diamond's *Guns, Germs & Steel: the Fate of Human Societies*
Jared Diamond's *Collapse: How Societies Choose to Fail or Survive*
E. E. Evans-Pritchard's *Witchcraft, Oracles and Magic Among the Azande*
James Ferguson's *The Anti-Politics Machine*
Clifford Geertz's *The Interpretation of Cultures*
David Graeber's *Debt: the First 5000 Years*
Karen Ho's *Liquidated: An Ethnography of Wall Street*
Geert Hofstede's *Culture's Consequences: Comparing Values, Behaviors, Institutes and Organizations across Nations*
Claude Lévi-Strauss's *Structural Anthropology*
Jay Macleod's *Ain't No Makin' It: Aspirations and Attainment in a Low-Income Neighborhood*
Saba Mahmood's *The Politics of Piety: The Islamic Revival and the Feminist Subject*
Marcel Mauss's *The Gift*

BUSINESS

Jean Lave & Etienne Wenger's *Situated Learning*
Theodore Levitt's *Marketing Myopia*
Burton G. Malkiel's *A Random Walk Down Wall Street*
Douglas McGregor's *The Human Side of Enterprise*
Michael Porter's *Competitive Strategy: Creating and Sustaining Superior Performance*
John Kotter's *Leading Change*
C. K. Prahalad & Gary Hamel's *The Core Competence of the Corporation*

CRIMINOLOGY

Michelle Alexander's *The New Jim Crow: Mass Incarceration in the Age of Colorblindness*
Michael R. Gottfredson & Travis Hirschi's *A General Theory of Crime*
Richard Herrnstein & Charles A. Murray's *The Bell Curve: Intelligence and Class Structure in American Life*
Elizabeth Loftus's *Eyewitness Testimony*
Jay Macleod's *Ain't No Makin' It: Aspirations and Attainment in a Low-Income Neighborhood*
Philip Zimbardo's *The Lucifer Effect*

ECONOMICS

Janet Abu-Lughod's *Before European Hegemony*
Ha-Joon Chang's *Kicking Away the Ladder*
David Brion Davis's *The Problem of Slavery in the Age of Revolution*
Milton Friedman's *The Role of Monetary Policy*
Milton Friedman's *Capitalism and Freedom*
David Graeber's *Debt: the First 5000 Years*
Friedrich Hayek's *The Road to Serfdom*
Karen Ho's *Liquidated: An Ethnography of Wall Street*

John Maynard Keynes's *The General Theory of Employment, Interest and Money*
Charles P. Kindleberger's *Manias, Panics and Crashes*
Robert Lucas's *Why Doesn't Capital Flow from Rich to Poor Countries?*
Burton G. Malkiel's *A Random Walk Down Wall Street*
Thomas Robert Malthus's *An Essay on the Principle of Population*
Karl Marx's *Capital*
Thomas Piketty's *Capital in the Twenty-First Century*
Amartya Sen's *Development as Freedom*
Adam Smith's *The Wealth of Nations*
Nassim Nicholas Taleb's *The Black Swan: The Impact of the Highly Improbable*
Amos Tversky's & Daniel Kahneman's *Judgment under Uncertainty: Heuristics and Biases*
Mahbub Ul Haq's *Reflections on Human Development*
Max Weber's *The Protestant Ethic and the Spirit of Capitalism*

FEMINISM AND GENDER STUDIES

Judith Butler's *Gender Trouble*
Simone De Beauvoir's *The Second Sex*
Michel Foucault's *History of Sexuality*
Betty Friedan's *The Feminine Mystique*
Saba Mahmood's *The Politics of Piety: The Islamic Revival and the Feminist Subject*
Joan Wallach Scott's *Gender and the Politics of History*
Mary Wollstonecraft's *A Vindication of the Rights of Woman*
Virginia Woolf's *A Room of One's Own*

GEOGRAPHY

The Brundtland Report's *Our Common Future*
Rachel Carson's *Silent Spring*
Charles Darwin's *On the Origin of Species*
James Ferguson's *The Anti-Politics Machine*
Jane Jacobs's *The Death and Life of Great American Cities*
James Lovelock's *Gaia: A New Look at Life on Earth*
Amartya Sen's *Development as Freedom*
Mathis Wackernagel & William Rees's *Our Ecological Footprint*

HISTORY

Janet Abu-Lughod's *Before European Hegemony*
Benedict Anderson's *Imagined Communities*
Bernard Bailyn's *The Ideological Origins of the American Revolution*
Hanna Batatu's *The Old Social Classes And The Revolutionary Movements Of Iraq*
Christopher Browning's *Ordinary Men: Reserve Police Batallion 101 and the Final Solution in Poland*
Edmund Burke's *Reflections on the Revolution in France*
William Cronon's *Nature's Metropolis: Chicago And The Great West*
Alfred W. Crosby's *The Columbian Exchange*
Hamid Dabashi's *Iran: A People Interrupted*
David Brion Davis's *The Problem of Slavery in the Age of Revolution*
Nathalie Zemon Davis's *The Return of Martin Guerre*
Jared Diamond's *Guns, Germs & Steel: the Fate of Human Societies*
Frank Dikotter's *Mao's Great Famine*
John W Dower's *War Without Mercy: Race And Power In The Pacific War*
W. E. B. Du Bois's *The Souls of Black Folk*
Richard J. Evans's *In Defence of History*
Lucien Febvre's *The Problem of Unbelief in the 16th Century*
Sheila Fitzpatrick's *Everyday Stalinism*

Eric Foner's *Reconstruction: America's Unfinished Revolution, 1863-1877*
Michel Foucault's *Discipline and Punish*
Michel Foucault's *History of Sexuality*
Francis Fukuyama's *The End of History and the Last Man*
John Lewis Gaddis's *We Now Know: Rethinking Cold War History*
Ernest Gellner's *Nations and Nationalism*
Eugene Genovese's *Roll, Jordan, Roll: The World the Slaves Made*
Carlo Ginzburg's *The Night Battles*
Daniel Goldhagen's *Hitler's Willing Executioners*
Jack Goldstone's *Revolution and Rebellion in the Early Modern World*
Antonio Gramsci's *The Prison Notebooks*
Alexander Hamilton, John Jay & James Madison's *The Federalist Papers*
Christopher Hill's *The World Turned Upside Down*
Carole Hillenbrand's *The Crusades: Islamic Perspectives*
Thomas Hobbes's *Leviathan*
Eric Hobsbawm's *The Age Of Revolution*
John A. Hobson's *Imperialism: A Study*
Albert Hourani's *History of the Arab Peoples*
Samuel P. Huntington's *The Clash of Civilizations and the Remaking of World Order*
C. L. R. James's *The Black Jacobins*
Tony Judt's *Postwar: A History of Europe Since 1945*
Ernst Kantorowicz's *The King's Two Bodies: A Study in Medieval Political Theology*
Paul Kennedy's *The Rise and Fall of the Great Powers*
Ian Kershaw's *The "Hitler Myth": Image and Reality in the Third Reich*
John Maynard Keynes's *The General Theory of Employment, Interest and Money*
Charles P. Kindleberger's *Manias, Panics and Crashes*
Martin Luther King Jr's *Why We Can't Wait*
Henry Kissinger's *World Order: Reflections on the Character of Nations and the Course of History*
Thomas Kuhn's *The Structure of Scientific Revolutions*
Georges Lefebvre's *The Coming of the French Revolution*
John Locke's *Two Treatises of Government*
Niccolò Machiavelli's *The Prince*
Thomas Robert Malthus's *An Essay on the Principle of Population*
Mahmood Mamdani's *Citizen and Subject: Contemporary Africa And The Legacy Of Late Colonialism*
Karl Marx's *Capital*
Stanley Milgram's *Obedience to Authority*
John Stuart Mill's *On Liberty*
Thomas Paine's *Common Sense*
Thomas Paine's *Rights of Man*
Geoffrey Parker's *Global Crisis: War, Climate Change and Catastrophe in the Seventeenth Century*
Jonathan Riley-Smith's *The First Crusade and the Idea of Crusading*
Jean-Jacques Rousseau's *The Social Contract*
Joan Wallach Scott's *Gender and the Politics of History*
Theda Skocpol's *States and Social Revolutions*
Adam Smith's *The Wealth of Nations*
Timothy Snyder's *Bloodlands: Europe Between Hitler and Stalin*
Sun Tzu's *The Art of War*
Keith Thomas's *Religion and the Decline of Magic*
Thucydides's *The History of the Peloponnesian War*
Frederick Jackson Turner's *The Significance of the Frontier in American History*
Odd Arne Westad's *The Global Cold War: Third World Interventions And The Making Of Our Times*

LITERATURE

Chinua Achebe's *An Image of Africa: Racism in Conrad's Heart of Darkness*
Roland Barthes's *Mythologies*
Homi K. Bhabha's *The Location of Culture*
Judith Butler's *Gender Trouble*
Simone De Beauvoir's *The Second Sex*
Ferdinand De Saussure's *Course in General Linguistics*
T. S. Eliot's *The Sacred Wood: Essays on Poetry and Criticism*
Zora Neale Huston's *Characteristics of Negro Expression*
Toni Morrison's *Playing in the Dark: Whiteness in the American Literary Imagination*
Edward Said's *Orientalism*
Gayatri Chakravorty Spivak's *Can the Subaltern Speak?*
Mary Wollstonecraft's *A Vindication of the Rights of Women*
Virginia Woolf's *A Room of One's Own*

PHILOSOPHY

Elizabeth Anscombe's *Modern Moral Philosophy*
Hannah Arendt's *The Human Condition*
Aristotle's *Metaphysics*
Aristotle's *Nicomachean Ethics*
Edmund Gettier's *Is Justified True Belief Knowledge?*
Georg Wilhelm Friedrich Hegel's *Phenomenology of Spirit*
David Hume's *Dialogues Concerning Natural Religion*
David Hume's *The Enquiry for Human Understanding*
Immanuel Kant's *Religion within the Boundaries of Mere Reason*
Immanuel Kant's *Critique of Pure Reason*
Søren Kierkegaard's *The Sickness Unto Death*
Søren Kierkegaard's *Fear and Trembling*
C. S. Lewis's *The Abolition of Man*
Alasdair MacIntyre's *After Virtue*
Marcus Aurelius's *Meditations*
Friedrich Nietzsche's *On the Genealogy of Morality*
Friedrich Nietzsche's *Beyond Good and Evil*
Plato's *Republic*
Plato's *Symposium*
Jean-Jacques Rousseau's *The Social Contract*
Gilbert Ryle's *The Concept of Mind*
Baruch Spinoza's *Ethics*
Sun Tzu's *The Art of War*
Ludwig Wittgenstein's *Philosophical Investigations*

POLITICS

Benedict Anderson's *Imagined Communities*
Aristotle's *Politics*
Bernard Bailyn's *The Ideological Origins of the American Revolution*
Edmund Burke's *Reflections on the Revolution in France*
John C. Calhoun's *A Disquisition on Government*
Ha-Joon Chang's *Kicking Away the Ladder*
Hamid Dabashi's *Iran: A People Interrupted*
Hamid Dabashi's *Theology of Discontent: The Ideological Foundation of the Islamic Revolution in Iran*
Robert Dahl's *Democracy and its Critics*
Robert Dahl's *Who Governs?*
David Brion Davis's *The Problem of Slavery in the Age of Revolution*

The Macat Library By Discipline

Alexis De Tocqueville's *Democracy in America*
James Ferguson's *The Anti-Politics Machine*
Frank Dikotter's *Mao's Great Famine*
Sheila Fitzpatrick's *Everyday Stalinism*
Eric Foner's *Reconstruction: America's Unfinished Revolution, 1863-1877*
Milton Friedman's *Capitalism and Freedom*
Francis Fukuyama's *The End of History and the Last Man*
John Lewis Gaddis's *We Now Know: Rethinking Cold War History*
Ernest Gellner's *Nations and Nationalism*
David Graeber's *Debt: the First 5000 Years*
Antonio Gramsci's *The Prison Notebooks*
Alexander Hamilton, John Jay & James Madison's *The Federalist Papers*
Friedrich Hayek's *The Road to Serfdom*
Christopher Hill's *The World Turned Upside Down*
Thomas Hobbes's *Leviathan*
John A. Hobson's *Imperialism: A Study*
Samuel P. Huntington's *The Clash of Civilizations and the Remaking of World Order*
Tony Judt's *Postwar: A History of Europe Since 1945*
David C. Kang's *China Rising: Peace, Power and Order in East Asia*
Paul Kennedy's *The Rise and Fall of Great Powers*
Robert Keohane's *After Hegemony*
Martin Luther King Jr.'s *Why We Can't Wait*
Henry Kissinger's *World Order: Reflections on the Character of Nations and the Course of History*
John Locke's *Two Treatises of Government*
Niccolò Machiavelli's *The Prince*
Thomas Robert Malthus's *An Essay on the Principle of Population*
Mahmood Mamdani's *Citizen and Subject: Contemporary Africa And The Legacy Of Late Colonialism*
Karl Marx's *Capital*
John Stuart Mill's *On Liberty*
John Stuart Mill's *Utilitarianism*
Hans Morgenthau's *Politics Among Nations*
Thomas Paine's *Common Sense*
Thomas Paine's *Rights of Man*
Thomas Piketty's *Capital in the Twenty-First Century*
Robert D. Putman's *Bowling Alone*
John Rawls's *Theory of Justice*
Jean-Jacques Rousseau's *The Social Contract*
Theda Skocpol's *States and Social Revolutions*
Adam Smith's *The Wealth of Nations*
Sun Tzu's *The Art of War*
Henry David Thoreau's *Civil Disobedience*
Thucydides's *The History of the Peloponnesian War*
Kenneth Waltz's *Theory of International Politics*
Max Weber's *Politics as a Vocation*
Odd Arne Westad's *The Global Cold War: Third World Interventions And The Making Of Our Times*

POSTCOLONIAL STUDIES

Roland Barthes's *Mythologies*
Frantz Fanon's *Black Skin, White Masks*
Homi K. Bhabha's *The Location of Culture*
Gustavo Gutiérrez's *A Theology of Liberation*
Edward Said's *Orientalism*
Gayatri Chakravorty Spivak's *Can the Subaltern Speak?*

PSYCHOLOGY

Gordon Allport's *The Nature of Prejudice*
Alan Baddeley & Graham Hitch's *Aggression: A Social Learning Analysis*
Albert Bandura's *Aggression: A Social Learning Analysis*
Leon Festinger's *A Theory of Cognitive Dissonance*
Sigmund Freud's *The Interpretation of Dreams*
Betty Friedan's *The Feminine Mystique*
Michael R. Gottfredson & Travis Hirschi's *A General Theory of Crime*
Eric Hoffer's *The True Believer: Thoughts on the Nature of Mass Movements*
William James's *Principles of Psychology*
Elizabeth Loftus's *Eyewitness Testimony*
A. H. Maslow's *A Theory of Human Motivation*
Stanley Milgram's *Obedience to Authority*
Steven Pinker's *The Better Angels of Our Nature*
Oliver Sacks's *The Man Who Mistook His Wife For a Hat*
Richard Thaler & Cass Sunstein's *Nudge: Improving Decisions About Health, Wealth and Happiness*
Amos Tversky's *Judgment under Uncertainty: Heuristics and Biases*
Philip Zimbardo's *The Lucifer Effect*

SCIENCE

Rachel Carson's *Silent Spring*
William Cronon's *Nature's Metropolis: Chicago And The Great West*
Alfred W. Crosby's *The Columbian Exchange*
Charles Darwin's *On the Origin of Species*
Richard Dawkin's *The Selfish Gene*
Thomas Kuhn's *The Structure of Scientific Revolutions*
Geoffrey Parker's *Global Crisis: War, Climate Change and Catastrophe in the Seventeenth Century*
Mathis Wackernagel & William Rees's *Our Ecological Footprint*

SOCIOLOGY

Michelle Alexander's *The New Jim Crow: Mass Incarceration in the Age of Colorblindness*
Gordon Allport's *The Nature of Prejudice*
Albert Bandura's *Aggression: A Social Learning Analysis*
Hanna Batatu's *The Old Social Classes And The Revolutionary Movements Of Iraq*
Ha-Joon Chang's *Kicking Away the Ladder*
W. E. B. Du Bois's *The Souls of Black Folk*
Émile Durkheim's *On Suicide*
Frantz Fanon's *Black Skin, White Masks*
Frantz Fanon's *The Wretched of the Earth*
Eric Foner's *Reconstruction: America's Unfinished Revolution, 1863-1877*
Eugene Genovese's *Roll, Jordan, Roll: The World the Slaves Made*
Jack Goldstone's *Revolution and Rebellion in the Early Modern World*
Antonio Gramsci's *The Prison Notebooks*
Richard Herrnstein & Charles A Murray's *The Bell Curve: Intelligence and Class Structure in American Life*
Eric Hoffer's *The True Believer: Thoughts on the Nature of Mass Movements*
Jane Jacobs's *The Death and Life of Great American Cities*
Robert Lucas's *Why Doesn't Capital Flow from Rich to Poor Countries?*
Jay Macleod's *Ain't No Makin' It: Aspirations and Attainment in a Low Income Neighborhood*
Elaine May's *Homeward Bound: American Families in the Cold War Era*
Douglas McGregor's *The Human Side of Enterprise*
C. Wright Mills's *The Sociological Imagination*

Thomas Piketty's *Capital in the Twenty-First Century*
Robert D. Putman's *Bowling Alone*
David Riesman's *The Lonely Crowd: A Study of the Changing American Character*
Edward Said's *Orientalism*
Joan Wallach Scott's *Gender and the Politics of History*
Theda Skocpol's *States and Social Revolutions*
Max Weber's *The Protestant Ethic and the Spirit of Capitalism*

THEOLOGY

Augustine's *Confessions*
Benedict's *Rule of St Benedict*
Gustavo Gutiérrez's *A Theology of Liberation*
Carole Hillenbrand's *The Crusades: Islamic Perspectives*
David Hume's *Dialogues Concerning Natural Religion*
Immanuel Kant's *Religion within the Boundaries of Mere Reason*
Ernst Kantorowicz's *The King's Two Bodies: A Study in Medieval Political Theology*
Søren Kierkegaard's *The Sickness Unto Death*
C. S. Lewis's *The Abolition of Man*
Saba Mahmood's *The Politics of Piety: The Islamic Revival and the Feminist Subject*
Baruch Spinoza's *Ethics*
Keith Thomas's *Religion and the Decline of Magic*